MW01056663

Taste of Home

COOL &
creamy

SMOOTHIES, ICE CREAM TREATS & MORE!

Indulge in 212 frosty, creamy delights!

Sipped through a straw or savored bite by bite, the 212 luscious creations in the *Cool & Creamy* cookbook will make your taste buds dance. Featuring everything from refreshing smoothies to old-fashioned ice cream drinks, silky pudding pies to rich cheesecakes, and pretty parfaits to decadent trifles, this brand-new book lets you make dozens of melt-in-your-mouth sensations.

Each of the five chapters hosts a pleasing assortment of heavenly confections suitable for any occasion. On warm-weather days, cool off with a Honeydew Kiwi Cooler (p. 11) or Cherry Cranberry Shake (p. 31) from the "Smoothies & Shakes" chapter. Tangy Lemon Custard Ice Cream (p. 33)...smooth, chocolaty Macaroon Ice Cream Torte (p. 38)...classic Butter Pecan Ice Cream (p. 36)...everyone will scream for the frozen delights found in "Ice Cream & Frozen Treats."

For potlucks and picnics, you can't go wrong with the yummy selections in "Refrigerated Desserts," which stars fluffy Frosted Orange Pie (p. 58), decadent Creamy Candy Bar Dessert (p. 72), fresh-n-fruity Banana Berry Tarts (p. 73) and other sweet treats. When the event calls for something extra special, you'll find just the thing in the "Puddings, Parfaits & More" and "Company's Coming" chapters. One bite of the impressive Cappuccino Mousse Trifle (p. 77), delectable White Chocolate Cherry Parfaits (p. 89), fun-to-make Swiss Swirl Ice Cream Cake (p. 99) or elegant Ladyfinger Lemon Torte (p. 104) will have your guests begging for the recipe.

With clear and easy-to-follow instructions plus inspiring, colorful photos of every recipe, whipping up any of the no-bake indulgences is simple and fun! So grab a glass—or a spoon—and treat yourself to the enticing, tongue-tingling flavors in *Cool & Creamy*.

Reiman Media Group, Inc.

President and Chief Executive Officer: Mary G. Berner
President, Food & Entertaining: Suzanne M. Grimes
Senior Vice President, Editor in Chief: Catherine Cassidy
Vice President, Executive Editor/Books: Heidi Reuter Lloyd
Creative Director: Ardyth Cope
Editor: Jean Steiner
Senior Editor/Books: Mark Hagen
Associate Editor: Sara Lancaster
Art Director: Gretchen Trautman
Content Production Supervisor: Julie Wagner
Layout Designers: Catherine Fletcher
Kathy Crawford
Proofreaders: Julie Schnittka
Linne Bruskewitz
Editorial Assistant: Barb Czysz

Food Director: Diane Werner RD
Test Kitchen Manager: Karen Scales
Recipe Editors: Sue A. Jurack (Senior)
Mary King
Christine Rukavena
Recipe Asset System Manager: Coleen Martin
Test Kitchen Assistant: Rita Krajcir

Studio Photographers: Rob Hagen (Senior)
Dan Roberts
Jim Wieland
Lori Foy
Senior Food Stylist: Sarah Thompson
Food Stylist Assistants: Kaitlyn Basasie
Alynna Malson
Set Stylists: Jenny Bradley Vent (Seni
Dee Dee Jacq
Photo Studio Coordinator: Kathleen Swaney

Cover Photography: Jim Wieland (Photograph
Julie Hertzfeld (Food Sty
Jennifer Janz (Food Stylis
Jenny Bradley Vent (Set S

© 2008 Reiman Media Group, Inc.
5400 S. 60th Street, Greendale WI 53129

International Standard Book Number (10): 0-89821-688-5
International Standard Book Number (13): 978-0-89821-6
Library of Congress Control Number: 2007938923

All rights reserved.
Printed in China.

Pictured on front cover:
Blueberry Cheesecake Ice Cream (p. 36), Orange Pineapple Smo
(p. 29) and Creamy Lime Chiller (p. 13)

Pictured on back cover:
Black Forest Freezer Pie (p. 96)

Taste of Home
COOL & creamy

SMOOTHIES, ICE CREAM TREATS & MORE!

The *Cool & Creamy* cookbook makes a great gift for those who like to indulge their sweet tooth. To order additional copies, specify item number 37552 and send $15.99 (plus $4.99 shipping/processing for one book, $5.99 for two or more) to: Shop Taste of Home, Suite 152, P.O. Box 26820, Lehigh Valley PA 18002-6820. To order by credit card, call toll-free 1-800/880-3012.

CHAPTER 1
Smoothies & Shakes

Banana Berry Drink, 10

4

CHERRY YOGURT SMOOTHIES

Katie Sloan • CHARLOTTE, NORTH CAROLINA

"I add some canned pie filling to create this special smoothie, a favorite of mine. I think the cherries and banana are an awesome combination!"

PREP/TOTAL TIME: 5 minutes

1	cup cranberry juice
1	cup (8 ounces) cherry yogurt
1/2	cup cherry pie filling
1	medium ripe banana, cut into chunks
1	to 1-1/2 cups ice cubes

In a blender, combine all ingredients; cover and process until blended. Pour into chilled glasses; serve immediately.

YIELD: 4 servings

RHUBARB CHEESECAKE SMOOTHIES

Kathy Specht • CAMBRIA, CALIFORNIA

"We love smoothies, so there isn't much we don't use to make unusual combinations. Cream cheese adds an extra-special touch to this yummy concoction which our friends and family just love."

PREP: 20 minutes + cooling

2	cups diced fresh *or* frozen rhubarb
1/4	cup water
4	tablespoons honey, *divided*
1-1/2	cups vanilla ice cream
1	cup milk
1	cup frozen sweetened sliced strawberries
2	packages (3 ounces *each*) cream cheese, cubed
1/2	cup vanilla yogurt
1/4	cup confectioners' sugar
5	ice cubes

In a large saucepan, bring the rhubarb, water and 2 tablespoons honey to a boil. Reduce heat; cover and simmer for 5-10 minutes or until rhubarb is tender. Remove from the heat; cool to room temperature.

In a blender, combine the ice cream, milk, rhubarb mixture, strawberries, cream cheese, yogurt, confectioners' sugar, ice cubes and remaining honey. Cover and process for 1 minute or until smooth. Pour into chilled glasses; serve immediately.

YIELD: 6 servings

WATERMELON SMOOTHIES

Sandra Pichon • SLIDELL, LOUISIANA

"This is so good to sip on a hot day. The simple summer beverage is a snap to blend up."

PREP/TOTAL TIME: 10 minutes

6	cups coarsely chopped seedless watermelon
1	cup lemon sherbet
12	ice cubes

Place half of the watermelon in a blender; cover and process until smooth. Add half of the sherbet and ice; cover and process until smooth. Repeat with remaining ingredients. Pour into chilled glasses; serve immediately.

YIELD: 6 servings

PEACHES 'N' CREAM COOLER

Carol Gillespie ● CHAMBERSBURG, PENNSYLVANIA

"Here's a delicious way to cool off on a sultry summer evening. This creamy fruit drink is not too sweet but plenty refreshing. My family and friends love it!"

PREP/TOTAL TIME: 10 minutes

1	cup apricot nectar, chilled
1/2	cup unsweetened pineapple juice, chilled
1/2	cup half-and-half cream
1	tablespoon lemon juice
1	tablespoon honey
1	teaspoon vanilla extract
1/4	teaspoon almond extract
2	cups frozen sliced peaches
4	ice cubes
3/4	cup sparkling water, chilled

In a blender, combine the first nine ingredients; cover and process until smooth. Add sparkling water; cover and process until blended. Pour into chilled glasses; serve immediately.

YIELD: 4 servings

TROPICAL MILK SHAKES

DeEtta Rasmussen ● OGDEN, IOWA

"This fruity shake has a bold banana flavor. It's a tasty tradition to serve this beverage when the family is together."

PREP/TOTAL TIME: 10 minutes

3/4	cup milk
2	medium ripe bananas
3	cups vanilla ice cream, softened
1	can (8 ounces) chunk pineapple, undrained
2	tablespoons flaked coconut, toasted
2	tablespoons chopped pecans

In a blender, combine the milk, bananas, ice cream and pineapple; cover and process until smooth. Pour into chilled glasses. Top with coconut and pecans. Serve immediately.

YIELD: 5 servings

CHOCOLATE MALTS

Marion Lowery ● MEDFORD, OREGON

"I can whip up this decadent ice cream treat in just minutes. It's a favorite with kids of all ages, particularly after a day in the pool or for dessert after a hot summer barbecue."

PREP/TOTAL TIME: 10 minutes

3/4	cup milk
1/2	cup caramel ice cream topping
2	cups chocolate ice cream, softened
3	tablespoons malted milk powder
2	tablespoons chopped pecans
Grated chocolate, optional	

In a blender, combine the first five ingredients; cover and process until blended. Pour into chilled glasses. Sprinkle with grated chocolate if desired. Serve immediately.

YIELD: 2 servings

RASPBERRY SMOOTHIES

Heather Mate • Pitt Meadows, British Columbia

"This simple smoothie is a nutritious choice for anyone on the go. Raspberries and banana give the not-too-sweet sipper its pleasant flavor."

PREP/TOTAL TIME: 5 minutes

- 1 cup milk
- 1 cup fresh *or* frozen unsweetened raspberries
- 1 small ripe banana, cut into chunks
- 1/2 cup apple juice
- 1/2 cup raspberry yogurt

In a blender, combine all ingredients; cover and process until blended. Pour into chilled glasses; serve immediately.

YIELD: 3 servings

FRUITY RED SMOOTHIES

Beverly Coyde • Gasport, New York

"This thick, tangy drink combines the refreshing flavors of cranberries, raspberries and strawberries. Once you start sipping it, you can't stop!"

PREP/TOTAL TIME: 5 minutes

- 1 carton (8 ounces) strawberry yogurt
- 1/2 to 3/4 cup cranberry juice
- 1-1/2 cups frozen unsweetened strawberries, quartered
- 1 cup frozen unsweetened raspberries
- 1 to 1-1/2 teaspoons sugar

In a blender, combine yogurt and cranberry juice. Add the strawberries, raspberries and sugar; cover and process until blended. Pour into chilled glasses; serve immediately.

YIELD: 2 servings

MORNING FRUIT SHAKE

Taste of Home Test Kitchen

"In addition to offering an assortment of juices and milk, why not serve this refreshing beverage with your family's favorite fruit flavors? Your thirsty clan will savor it so much, you'll be asked to make it from sunrise to sundown!"

PREP/TOTAL TIME: 10 minutes

- 1 cup cranberry juice
- 2 medium ripe bananas, sliced
- 2 cartons (8 ounces *each*) raspberry yogurt *or* flavor of your choice
- 1 tablespoon confectioners' sugar

Few drops red food coloring
Mint leaves, optional

In a blender, combine the first five ingredients; cover and blend until smooth. Pour into a pitcher or chilled glasses; garnish with mint if desired. Serve immediately.

YIELD: 4 servings

CANTALOUPE COOLER

Ruth Andrewson ● LEAVENWORTH, WASHINGTON

"Strawberries, grapes and cantaloupe combine in this delightful drink which takes just seconds to whip up in the blender.**"**

PREP/TOTAL TIME: 5 minutes

> 1   cup cubed cantaloupe
> 1   cup frozen unsweetened strawberries
> 1   cup green grapes
> 1/2 cup ice cubes
> Sugar substitute equivalent to 4 teaspoons sugar

Place all ingredients in the order listed in a blender. Cover and process until smooth. Pour into chilled glasses; serve immediately.

YIELD: 4 servings

APRICOT PEACH SMOOTHIES

DeAnn Alleva ● HUDSON, WISCONSIN

"The mellow mingling of peach, banana and apricot flavors makes this refreshing smoothie so soothing. A spark of tart lemon adds a little tang, but honey keeps the drink on the lightly sweet side.**"**

PREP/TOTAL TIME: 10 minutes

> 1   can (5-1/2 ounces) apricot nectar
> 1   medium ripe banana, frozen and cut into chunks
> 1   cup (8 ounces) fat-free vanilla yogurt
> 2   cups sliced fresh *or* frozen unsweetened peaches
> 1   tablespoon lemon juice
> 1   tablespoon honey
> 1   teaspoon grated lemon peel
> 6   ice cubes

In a blender, combine all ingredients. Cover and process until smooth. Pour into chilled glasses; serve immediately.

YIELD: 4 servings

CAPPUCCINO SMOOTHIES

Michelle Cluney ● LAKE MARY, FLORIDA

"Topped with miniature marshmallows, this icy cappuccino beverage is a twist on traditional fruit smoothies. My mom and I created it when trying to fix an easy snack.**"**

PREP/TOTAL TIME: 5 minutes

> 1   cup (8 ounces) cappuccino *or* coffee yogurt
> 1/3 cup milk
> 3   tablespoons confectioners' sugar, optional
> 1   tablespoon chocolate syrup
> 1-1/2 cups ice cubes
> 1/2 cup miniature marshmallows, *divided*

In a blender, combine the yogurt, milk, sugar if desired and chocolate syrup. Add ice cubes and 1/4 cup marshmallows; cover and process until blended. Pour into chilled glasses; top with the remaining marshmallows. Serve immediately.

YIELD: 3 servings

PEAR COOLER

Jeri Clayton
SANDY, UTAH

"My daughter and I had eaten a cold fruit soup while on vacation. When we got home, we tried to create our own version—and wound up with this yummy smoothie. Everyone enjoys it."

PREP/TOTAL TIME: 5 minutes

1	can (15-1/4 ounces) sliced pears, undrained
2	cups ice cubes
1	envelope whipped topping mix
1/4	to 1/2 teaspoon vanilla *or* almond extract, optional

In a blender, combine all of the ingredients. Cover and process until smooth. Pour into chilled glasses; serve immediately.

YIELD: 3 servings

BANANA BERRY DRINK

Eric Knoben ● EDGEWOOD, WASHINGTON

❝*This cold, refreshing beverage is a great substitute for breakfast when you're in a hurry. Just fill a glass and go!*❞

PREP/TOTAL TIME: 10 minutes

- 3/4 cup orange juice, chilled
- 1/3 cup pineapple juice, chilled
- 1 cup frozen blueberries
- 1/2 cup frozen sweetened sliced strawberries
- 1/2 cup plain yogurt
- 1 small ripe banana, sliced

Place half of each ingredient in a blender; cover and process until smooth. Pour into chilled glasses. Repeat with remaining ingredients. Serve immediately.

YIELD: 5 servings

STRAWBERRY LEMONADE SLUSH

Sue Jorgensen ● RAPID CITY, SOUTH DAKOTA

❝*This fruity slush really perks up the taste buds. I have made it for Christmas, Valentine's Day, summer potlucks and other occasions, and there is seldom any left.*❞

PREP: 5 minutes + freezing

- 1 package (10 ounces) frozen sweetened sliced strawberries, thawed
- 3/4 cup pink lemonade concentrate
- 3/4 cup water
- 3/4 cup ice cubes
- 1 cup club soda

In a blender, combine the strawberries, lemonade concentrate, water and ice cubes. Cover and process until smooth. Pour into a freezer container. Cover and freeze for at least 12 hours or up to 3 months.

Let stand at room temperature for 1 hour before serving. Stir in club soda. Pour into chilled glasses; serve immediately.

YIELD: 4 servings

SPRINGTIME LIME SLUSHY

Joyce Minge-Johns ● JACKSONVILLE, FLORIDA

❝*I rely on a handful of ingredients to fix this lively lime beverage. With its tangy flavor and slushy consistency, it's especially refreshing.*❞

PREP: 10 minutes + freezing

- 2 packages (3 ounces *each*) lime gelatin
- 2 cups boiling water
- 2 cups cold water
- 2 quarts lime sherbet
- 3 cups ginger ale, chilled

In a freezer container, dissolve gelatin in boiling water. Stir in the cold water and sherbet until combined. Freeze for 4 hours or until set.

Remove from the freezer 45 minutes before serving. For each serving, place 1 cup of slush mixture in a glass; add about 1/3 cup ginger ale.

YIELD: 8 servings

TROPICAL FRUIT DRINK

Janet Eggers ● SURING, WISCONSIN

"This yummy thirst-quencher with its smoothie-like texture stars strawberries, kiwifruit and mango. Pour your kids tall glasses— it's a good way to get them to eat fruit."

PREP/TOTAL TIME: 5 minutes

1-1/2   cups orange juice
1   cup halved strawberries
1   medium mango, peeled, pitted and cut into chunks
2   medium kiwifruit, peeled and quartered
1   tablespoon honey
14   ice cubes
1/2   cup chilled club soda

In a blender, combine the first five ingredients; cover and process until smooth. Add ice cubes; cover and process until blended. Stir in soda. Pour into chilled tall glasses; serve immediately.

YIELD: 4 servings

HONEYDEW KIWI COOLER

Taste of Home Test Kitchen

"We suggest you make a big pitcher of this thick, fruity beverage because guests are sure to ask for a second glass! The colorful quencher has a refreshing melon flavor and gets its creamy consistency from fat-free yogurt."

PREP/TOTAL TIME: 5 minutes

3   cups cubed honeydew
2   kiwifruit, peeled and cubed
1/2   cup fat-free plain yogurt
2   tablespoons honey
1   cup ice cubes
2   to 3 drops green food coloring

In a blender, combine all ingredients; cover and process until blended. Pour into chilled glasses; serve immediately.

YIELD: 4 servings

STRAWBERRY SMOOTHIES

Emma Birchenough ● LOWVILLE, NEW YORK

"For a light breakfast all by itself, this creamy concoction will hit the spot! It also makes a super snack in the afternoon."

PREP/TOTAL TIME: 10 minutes

1   carton (8 ounces) strawberry yogurt
1   cup milk
1/2   cup unsweetened frozen strawberries
1   tablespoon honey
1   pint vanilla ice cream
1   medium ripe banana, quartered
Red food coloring

Place all ingredients in a blender; cover and process until smooth. Pour into chilled glasses; serve immediately.

YIELD: 4 servings

BLUEBERRY FRUIT SMOOTHIES

Mary Walton
WOODLAND, WASHINGTON

"This low-fat but yummy smoothie just might take you back to soda fountain days!"

PREP/TOTAL TIME: 5 minutes

1 cup reduced-fat vanilla ice cream
1 cup fresh *or* frozen blueberries
1/2 cup chopped fresh *or* frozen peaches, thawed
1/2 cup pineapple juice
1/4 cup reduced-fat vanilla yogurt

In a blender, combine all the ingredients; cover and process until smooth. Pour into chilled glasses; serve immediately.

YIELD: 3 servings

CREAMY LIME CHILLER

Maria Regakis ● SOMERVILLE, MASSACHUSETTS

"This frosty refresher always hits the spot. Neither too sweet nor too tart, this pretty pick-me-up will perk up any special occasion."

PREP/TOTAL TIME: 5 minutes

1	cup milk
1	cup lime sherbet
1/4	cup limeade concentrate

Yellow food coloring

Place all ingredients in a blender; cover and process until smooth. Pour into chilled glasses; serve immediately.

YIELD: 2 servings

BANANA SPLIT SMOOTHIES

Darlene Brenden ● SALEM, OREGON

"This smooth and creamy beverage tastes just like a banana split. It's easy to blend together so it's great any time of day."

PREP/TOTAL TIME: 15 minutes

2	medium ripe bananas
1	can (8 ounces) crushed pineapple, drained
1-1/2	cups milk
1/2	cup fresh *or* frozen unsweetened sliced strawberries
2	tablespoons honey
5	ice cubes

Whipped topping, chocolate syrup and maraschino cherries

In a blender, combine the first five ingredients; cover and process until smooth. Gradually add ice, blending until slushy. Pour into chilled glasses. Garnish with whipped topping, chocolate syrup and cherries. Serve immediately.

YIELD: 4 servings

PEACHY ORANGE SHAKES

Helen Phillips ● HORSEHEADS, NEW YORK

"I found this recipe in an old cookbook I bought at a garage sale. I liked the ingredients, and when I tried the shake, I decided it was a keeper."

PREP/TOTAL TIME: 10 minutes

1	can (8 ounces) sliced peaches
1	cup orange juice
2	cups vanilla ice cream, softened
1	tablespoon peach yogurt
1	tablespoon milk

Drain peaches, reserving syrup; save half of the peaches and syrup for another use.

In a blender, combine the orange juice, ice cream, yogurt, milk, half of the peaches and 1 tablespoon syrup (add any remaining syrup to the reserved peaches). Cover and process until smooth. Pour into chilled glasses; serve immediately.

YIELD: 2-3 servings

PINEAPPLE SUNRISE SMOOTHIES

Diana Mueller ● LAS VEGAS, NEVADA

"This great-tasting beverage is an easy way to get kids to eat their fruit. It's perfect for breakfast, but my gang likes it throughout the day."

PREP/TOTAL TIME: 5 minutes

1 can (14 ounces) unsweetened pineapple tidbits
1 small ripe banana, sliced
3/4 cup fresh *or* frozen raspberries
2 tablespoons sugar
2 ice cubes

Drain pineapple, reserving juice and 1 cup pineapple (refrigerate remaining pineapple for another use).

In a blender, combine the pineapple juice, pineapple, banana, raspberries, sugar and ice; cover and process until smooth. Stir if necessary. Pour into chilled glasses; serve immediately.

YIELD: 2 servings

TWO-FRUIT FROSTY

Angie Hansen ● GILDFORD, MONTANA

"This is a refreshing and colorful drink to serve for brunch. The cinnamon and nutmeg give it just the right amount of zing."

PREP/TOTAL TIME: 10 minutes

1-1/2 cups fresh *or* frozen blueberries *or* huckleberries
1 cup frozen unsweetened sliced peaches, thawed
1 cup milk
1 cup (8 ounces) vanilla yogurt
1/4 to 1/3 cup honey
1/2 teaspoon ground cinnamon
1/2 teaspoon ground nutmeg
Cinnamon sticks, optional

In a blender, combine the blueberries, peaches and milk; cover and process on high. Add the yogurt, honey, cinnamon and nutmeg; cover and blend until smooth. Pour into chilled glasses. Garnish with cinnamon sticks if desired. Serve immediately.

YIELD: 4 servings

RUBY-RED STRAWBERRY BURST

Romaine Wetzel ● RONKS, PENNSYLVANIA

"My friend served this beverage when I was her guest one warm summer day. It's tasty and easy to prepare."

PREP/TOTAL TIME: 5 minutes

2 cups red grapefruit and strawberry juice drink
1 medium firm banana, cut into chunks
6 fresh strawberries
1 cup ice cubes
1 teaspoon sugar

In a blender, combine all ingredients; cover and process until smooth. Pour into chilled glasses; serve immediately.

YIELD: 2 servings

STRAWBERRY PEACH SMOOTHIES

Taste of Home Test Kitchen

"Instead of pouring a glass of ordinary orange juice, why not whip up this refreshing smoothie that's quickly prepared in a blender. It's a great start to any day."

PREP/TOTAL TIME: 10 minutes

- 2 cups milk
- 1 cup frozen unsweetened peach slices
- 1 cup frozen unsweetened strawberries
- 1/4 cup orange juice
- 2 tablespoons honey

In a blender, combine all ingredients. Cover and process until smooth. Pour into chilled glasses; serve immediately.

YIELD: 4 servings

MELON FRUIT SLUSH

Jane Walker ● DEWEY, ARIZONA

"This pretty pink drink features fresh honeydew and cantaloupe as well as luscious pineapple, strawberries and bananas."

Prep: 15 minutes + freezing

- 1 can (20 ounces) crushed pineapple, undrained
- 1 container (10 ounces) frozen sweetened sliced strawberries
- 4 medium ripe bananas, cut into chunks
- 1 cup cubed cantaloupe
- 1 cup cubed honeydew
- 2-1/2 cups water
- 3/4 cup orange juice concentrate
- 3/4 cup lemonade concentrate
- 6 liters lemon-lime soda, chilled

In a blender, process the fruit in batches until smooth. Pour into a 3-qt. freezer container. Stir in the water and concentrates. Cover and freeze until icy. To serve, spoon 1/2 cup into a glass; add about 1 cup soda.

YIELD: 20-25 servings

RASPBERRY CREAM SMOOTHIES

Nicki Woods ● SPRINGFIELD, MISSOURI

"These thick, creamy smoothies are a satisfying and healthy snack that is sure to be popular whenever you serve it."

PREP/TOTAL TIME: 10 minutes

- 2 cups orange juice
- 2 cups fat-free reduced-sugar raspberry yogurt
- 2 cups frozen vanilla yogurt
- 2 small ripe bananas, cut into chunks and frozen (1 cup)
- 3 cups frozen raspberries
- 2 teaspoons vanilla extract

In a blender, cover and process the ingredients in batches until blended. Stir if necessary. Pour into chilled glasses; serve immediately.

YIELD: 6 servings

CREAMY MANDARIN COOLER

Renee Richardson ● POUNDING MILL, VIRGINIA

"This frothy and flavorful concoction is as fast to make as it is to refresh. It's delicious at breakfast or any other time of day, and it tastes just like an old-fashioned Dreamsicle."

PREP/TOTAL TIME: 5 minutes

- 3/4 cup fat-free milk
- 1/4 cup orange juice
- 1 can (11 ounces) mandarin oranges, undrained
- 1 carton (6 ounces) fat-free reduced-sugar orange creme yogurt
- 1 package (1 ounce) sugar-free instant vanilla pudding mix
- 12 to 15 ice cubes

In a blender, combine all ingredients; cover and process for 20 seconds or until smooth. Stir if necessary. Pour into chilled glasses; serve immediately.

YIELD: 5 servings

COOL WATERS SHAKES

Taste of Home Test Kitchen

"Ride a wave of approval when you serve this refreshing berry-flavored beverage. Kids will love its pastel blue color and sea-foamy consistency...and with just three simple ingredients, it's a breeze to whip up in the blender."

PREP/TOTAL TIME: 10 minutes

- 4 cups cold milk
- 2 packages (3 ounces *each*) berry blue gelatin
- 4 cups vanilla ice cream

In a blender, combine 2 cups of milk, one package of gelatin and 2 cups of ice cream. Cover and process for 30 seconds or until smooth. Repeat with remaining ingredients. Pour into glasses; serve immediately.

YIELD: 6 servings

CHOCOLATE BANANA SMOOTHIES

Katherine Lipka ● GALESBURG, MICHIGAN

"Instant pudding makes a wonderful, creamy chocolate drink when blended with some frozen banana. It's fun, tasty and easy."

PREP/TOTAL TIME: 5 minutes

- 2 cups cold 2% milk
- 1 package (1.4 ounces) sugar-free instant chocolate pudding mix
- 2 tablespoons vanilla extract
- 2 large ripe frozen bananas, sliced
- 2 cups coarsely crushed ice cubes

In a blender, combine the milk, pudding mix and vanilla; cover and process until blended. Add the bananas and ice; cover and process until smooth. Pour into chilled glasses; serve immediately.

YIELD: 4 servings

FRUITY SUMMER COOLER

Ruth Andrewson
LEAVENWORTH, WASHINGTON

"*When the melons first come in, we make this delightful, thirst-quenching cooler. Cantaloupe and pineapple are a great combination.*"

PREP/TOTAL TIME: 10 minutes

6	to 8 ice cubes
1/2	cup cubed cantaloupe
1/2	cup pineapple chunks
1/2	cup cranberry juice
1/3	cup sliced banana
1/4	cup pineapple juice
1	tablespoon honey
3/4	teaspoon lemon juice
1/4	teaspoon grated lemon peel

In a blender, combine all the ingredients; cover and process until smooth. Pour into chilled glasses; serve immediately.

YIELD: 2-3 servings

SUNRISE SLUSHIES

Linda Evancoe-Coble • LEOLA, PENNSYLVANIA

"My teenage daughters are perpetual dieters, so I worry about their nutrition. I came up with this yummy breakfast beverage full of fruity goodness, and they love it."

PREP/TOTAL TIME: 10 minutes

- 2 cups orange juice
- 1 cup reduced-calorie reduced-sugar cranberry juice
- 1 medium tart apple, coarsely chopped
- 1/2 cup cubed peeled mango
- 2 kiwifruit, peeled, sliced and quartered
- 2 cups halved fresh strawberries
- 8 to 10 ice cubes

In a blender, place half of each ingredient; cover and process until smooth. Pour into chilled glasses. Repeat with remaining ingredients. Serve immediately.

YIELD: 8 servings

PEACH SMOOTHIES

Martha Polasek • MARKHAM, TEXAS

"Whip up this creamy concoction as a refreshing and nutritious snack or a quick chilled breakfast. Because you can use frozen fruit, you don't have to wait until peaches are in season to enjoy this delicious drink."

PREP/TOTAL TIME: 5 minutes

- 1/2 cup peach *or* apricot nectar
- 1/2 cup sliced fresh *or* frozen peaches
- 1/4 cup vanilla yogurt
- 2 ice cubes

In a blender, combine all ingredients. Cover and process until blended. Pour into chilled glasses; serve immediately.

YIELD: 2 servings

MINT MOCHA SHAKES

Edna Hoffman • HEBRON, INDIANA

"Cool off with this yummy ice cream drink that delightfully blends chocolate, coffee and mint flavors."

PREP/TOTAL TIME: 5 minutes

- 2 cups milk
- 1 teaspoon vanilla extract
- 1/8 teaspoon mint extract
- 1 envelope (.77 ounce) instant cappuccino Irish cream mix
- 2 cups chocolate ice cream, softened

In a blender, combine all ingredients; cover and process until blended. Stir if necessary. Pour into chilled glasses; serve immediately.

YIELD: 4 servings

VERY BERRY SMOOTHIES

Bonnie Roher • WRANGELL, ALASKA

"We live on a remote side of an island in southeastern Alaska where blueberries are abundant. I use these and other berries as many ways as possible all summer long. These smoothies are scrumptious."

PREP/TOTAL TIME: 5 minutes

2	cartons (6 ounces *each*) blueberry yogurt
1/4	cup grape juice
1-1/2	cups frozen blueberries
1	cup frozen blackberries

Sugar substitute equivalent to
2 tablespoons sugar

In a blender, place all ingredients in the order listed; cover and process until blended. Pour into chilled glasses; serve immediately.

YIELD: 4 servings

TROPICAL SMOOTHIES

Wendy Thomas • PICKENS, SOUTH CAROLINA

"We like to experiment with different kinds of smoothies, and this refreshing creation is our favorite so far. The thick, creamy blend has fabulous fruit flavors. Serve it as a day-starter or afternoon pick-me-up."

PREP/TOTAL TIME: 10 minutes

2	cartons (6 ounces *each*) pina colada *or* pineapple yogurt
1	cup milk
1	can (11 ounces) mandarin oranges, drained
1/2	small ripe banana
1/2	cup frozen peach slices
2	tablespoons plus 1-1/2 teaspoons instant vanilla pudding mix
17	to 20 ice cubes

In a blender, combine the first six ingredients; cover and process until smooth. While processing, add a few ice cubes at a time until mixture achieves desired thickness. Pour into chilled glasses; serve immediately.

YIELD: 5 servings

PEAR SLUSHY

Darlene Brenden • SALEM, OREGON

"Pears may not be a typical smoothie ingredient, but they sure lend a special touch to this drink. The recipe is so easy to double for guests, too."

PREP/TOTAL TIME: 5 minutes

1	cup chopped peeled ripe pear
1/4	cup orange juice
1/4	cup unsweetened pineapple juice
2	tablespoons honey
6	ice cubes

In a blender, combine all ingredients; cover and process until smooth. Pour into chilled glasses; serve immediately.

YIELD: 2 servings

ORANGE STRAWBERRY SMOOTHIES

Jan Gilreath
WINNEBAGO, MINNESOTA

"My family and friends were so surprised when I told them that this refreshing, healthy drink has a secret ingredient...tofu! My dad often requests it for dessert."

PREP/TOTAL TIME: 5 minutes

2-1/4	cups orange juice
1	package (12.3 ounces) silken reduced-fat firm tofu
3	cups halved frozen unsweetened strawberries
1-1/2	cups sliced ripe bananas

In a food processor, combine the orange juice, tofu, strawberries and bananas; cover and pulse until blended. Pour into chilled glasses; serve immediately.

YIELD: 6 servings

BERRY SMOOTHIES

Patricia Mahoney ● Presque Isle, Maine

"Add a blush of color and a burst of frosty berry flavor to your meal with these scrumptious, summery smoothies."

Prep/Total Time: 5 minutes

- 2/3 cup milk
- 3/4 cup frozen unsweetened strawberries
- 1/3 cup frozen unsweetened raspberries
- 2 tablespoons sugar
- 3/4 cup ice cubes

Place the milk, berries and sugar in a blender; cover and process until blended. Add ice cubes; cover and process until smooth. Pour into chilled glasses; serve immediately.

Yield: 2 servings

FROSTY LEMON DRINK

Taste of Home Test Kitchen

"In the heat of summer, you'll find yourself making this tart-tasting beverage often. Serve it as a light dessert or midday snack."

Prep/Total Time: 10 minutes

- 3/4 cup lemonade concentrate
- 1/2 cup nonfat dry milk powder
- 1/3 cup sugar
- 3/4 cup cold water
- 1/8 teaspoon almond extract
- 16 to 18 ice cubes
- 3 drops yellow food coloring, optional

In a blender, combine the first five ingredients; cover and process until blended. Add ice cubes, a few at a time; cover and process until slushy. Add food coloring if desired. Pour into chilled glasses; serve immediately.

Yield: 4 servings

YOGURT BREAKFAST DRINK

Renee Gastineau ● Seattle, Washington

"Sleepy heads will savor this dreamy smoothie. Simply blend yogurt, milk and orange juice concentrate for a fresh start to your day."

Prep/Total Time: 5 minutes

- 2 cups (16 ounces) reduced-fat vanilla yogurt
- 2 cups (16 ounces) reduced-fat peach yogurt
- 1/2 cup frozen orange juice concentrate
- 1/2 cup fat-free milk
- 2 cups ice cubes

In a blender, combine the first four ingredients; cover and process until smooth. Add ice cubes; cover and process until smooth. Pour into glasses; serve immediately.

Yield: 6 servings

PINEAPPLE SMOOTHIES

Darlene Brenden • SALEM, OREGON

"This cool, quick beverage reminds me of our visits to the Hawaiian Islands. It's a not-too-sweet smoothie that's sure to refresh any time of day."

PREP/TOTAL TIME: 10 minutes

1-1/2 cups unsweetened pineapple
juice
1 cup 1% buttermilk
2 cups ice cubes
2 cans (8 ounces *each*)
unsweetened crushed pineapple
1/4 cup sugar

In a blender, combine all ingredients; cover and process until smooth. Pour into chilled glasses; serve immediately.

YIELD: 6 servings

BLACKBERRY BANANA SMOOTHIES

Heidi Butts • STREETSBORO, OHIO

"I originally began blending up this simple beverage when our young girls shied away from berries. Now they're thrilled whenever I serve it! The thick, fruity drink is a refreshing treat no matter what kind of berries you use."

PREP/TOTAL TIME: 15 minutes

2 cups orange juice
1/3 cup vanilla yogurt
2 medium ripe bananas, cut into
thirds and frozen
1/2 cup fresh *or* frozen blackberries

In a blender, combine all ingredients. Cover and process until blended. Pour into chilled glasses; serve immediately.

YIELD: 4 servings

FOUR-FRUIT SMOOTHIES

Kathleen Tribble • SANTA YNEZ, CALIFORNIA

"Kids will be glad to sip this cool and tangy treat, and you'll be glad to know it's full of good-for-you fruit!"

PREP/TOTAL TIME: 10 minutes

1 cup orange juice
1 package (10 ounces) frozen
sweetened raspberries, partially
thawed
1 cup frozen unsweetened
strawberries
1 medium ripe banana, cut into
chunks
6 ice cubes
1 to 2 tablespoons sugar

In a blender, combine all ingredients. Cover and process until smooth. Pour into chilled glasses; serve immediately.

YIELD: 4 servings

CREAMY ORANGE DRINK

Julie Curfman ● CHEHALIS, WASHINGTON

"This frothy orange drink is a real treat as a snack, for a holiday breakfast or at a special brunch. I love the combination of orange and cream!"

PREP/TOTAL TIME: 10 minutes

- 6 cups orange juice, *divided*
- 1/2 teaspoon vanilla extract
- 1 package (3.4 ounces) instant vanilla pudding mix
- 1 envelope whipped topping mix

In a small mixing bowl, combine 3 cups orange juice, vanilla, and the pudding and whipped topping mixes; beat until smooth. Stir in remaining orange juice. Pour into chilled glasses; serve immediately.

YIELD: 6 servings

LEMON PINEAPPLE SMOOTHIES

Brook Kaske ● ROCHESTER, MINNESOTA

"Five ingredients and a few moments are all you need to fix this citrus specialty. I originally came up with the recipe to use up leftover pineapple. It's a great dessert on a warm evening."

PREP/TOTAL TIME: 5 minutes

- 2 cups vanilla ice cream
- 1 can (20 ounces) pineapple tidbits, drained
- 1 cup chilled lemon-lime soda
- 2 tablespoons lemonade concentrate
- 1 drop yellow food coloring

In a blender, combine all ingredients; cover and process until smooth. Pour into chilled glasses; serve immediately.

YIELD: 4 servings

FRUIT SMOOTHIES

Bryce Sickich ● NEW PORT RICHEY, FLORIDA

"I created this six-ingredient recipe when experimenting in the kitchen one day. The smoothies make a wholesome, nutrition-packed snack."

PREP/TOTAL TIME: 5 minutes

- 3/4 cup fat-free milk
- 1/2 cup orange juice
- 1/2 cup unsweetened applesauce
- 1 small ripe banana, halved
- 1/2 cup frozen unsweetened raspberries
- 7 to 10 ice cubes

In a blender, combine all ingredients; cover and process until smooth. Pour into chilled glasses; serve immediately.

YIELD: 3 servings

CRANSATIONAL BREAKFAST DRINK

Amanda Schafer ● PERRYVILLE, MISSOURI

"I frequently whip up this colorful beverage for breakfast. The smoothie is a fast treat on any morning."

PREP/TOTAL TIME: 10 minutes

- 4 cups orange juice
- 2 medium firm bananas, cut into chunks
- 1-1/2 cups frozen cranberries
- 1/4 cup 2% milk
- 1/4 cup sugar
- 4 ice cubes

In a blender, place half of the orange juice, bananas, cranberries, milk, sugar and ice cubes; cover and process until smooth. Pour into a pitcher or chilled glasses. Repeat with remaining ingredients. Serve immediately.

YIELD: 8 servings

PEPPERMINT CHOCOLATE MALT

Carol Gillespie ● CHAMBERSBURG, PENNSYLVANIA

"I'm an avid recipe contestant entrant. I concocted this recipe, and my family and friends absolutely love these thick and minty ice cream malts."

PREP/TOTAL TIME: 10 minutes

- 3 cups chocolate milk
- 4 cups vanilla ice cream, *divided*
- 1/3 cup plus 1-1/2 teaspoons malted milk powder, *divided*
- 2 tablespoons chocolate syrup
- 1/2 teaspoon peppermint extract
- 1/8 teaspoon ground cinnamon
- Crushed peppermint candy and variegated mint leaves, optional

In a blender, combine the milk, 2 cups ice cream, 1/3 cup malted milk powder, chocolate syrup, extract and cinnamon. Cover and process until smooth. Pour into chilled glasses. Top each with a scoop of the remaining ice cream. Sprinkle with the remaining malted milk powder. Garnish each glass with candy and mint leaves if desired. Serve immediately.

YIELD: 5 servings

THICK FRUIT WHIP

Nancy Zimmerman ● CAPE MAY COURT HOUSE, NEW JERSEY

"This is a refreshing drink that combines the great tastes of bananas and strawberries. I've experimented with other fruit combinations, so this recipe can be adapted."

PREP/TOTAL TIME: 10 minutes

- 1 can (14 ounces) sweetened condensed milk
- 2 cups sliced unsweetened strawberries
- 1 medium firm banana
- 1/4 cup lemon juice
- 2 cups ice cubes

In a food processor or blender, combine all of the ingredients. Cover and process until smooth. Pour into glasses; serve immediately.

YIELD: 4 servings

RASPBERRY LEMON SMOOTHIES

Taste of Home
Test Kitchen

"A cool, tangy thirst-quencher, this sure hits the spot on a hot day! It's not too thick—more like a punch—and perfect for parties."

PREP: 15 minutes + chilling

  2 **cups boiling water**
  8 **lemon herbal tea bags**
  2 **cups pineapple juice**
  1 **pint raspberry sherbet**
Lemon slices, optional

In a teapot, pour boiling water over tea bags; cover and steep for 5 minutes. Discard bags. Chill tea.

In a blender, cover and process the tea, pineapple juice and sherbet until smooth. Pour into glasses. Garnish with lemon if desired. Serve immediately.

YIELD: 4 servings

SO-HEALTHY SMOOTHIES

Jessica Gerschitz • JERICHO, NEW YORK

"This tastes like a milk shake, but it doesn't have all the guilt or fat. My husband and I look forward to it every day for breakfast. It's so good for you and will keep you energized for hours."

PREP/TOTAL TIME: 15 minutes

- 1 **cup fat-free milk**
- 1/4 **cup orange juice**
- 2 **tablespoons vanilla yogurt**
- 1 **tablespoon honey**
- 1 **small banana, sliced and frozen**
- 2/3 **cup frozen blueberries**
- 1/2 **cup chopped peeled mango, frozen**
- 1/4 **cup frozen unsweetened peach slices**

In a blender, combine all ingredients; cover and process until smooth. Pour into chilled glasses; serve immediately.

YIELD: 4 servings

SUNNY SLUSH

Carol Wakley • NORTH EAST, PENNSYLVANIA

"A few years ago, I hosted a Hawaiian luau. As guests arrived, we sipped on this refreshing slush I stirred up. What a great way to start the party!"

PREP/TOTAL TIME: 10 minutes

- 6 **cups pineapple juice**
- 4 **pints lemon sherbet**
- 24 **ice cubes**
- 1 **teaspoon rum extract**

In a blender, combine pineapple juice, sherbet, ice and extract in batches; cover and process until smooth. Pour into chilled glasses; serve immediately.

YIELD: 12 servings

BLUEBERRY ORANGE SMOOTHIES

Nella Parker • HERSEY, MICHIGAN

"Start out your mornings with one of these refreshing smoothies using low fat dairy products and blueberries."

Prep/Total Time: 10 minutes

- 2 **medium navel oranges**
- 1 **cup fat-free plain yogurt**
- 1/4 **cup fat-free milk**
- 2/3 **cup fresh or frozen blueberries**
- 4 **teaspoons sugar**
- 1 **to 1-1/3 cups ice cubes**

Peel and remove the white pith from oranges; separate into sections. Place in a blender; add the yogurt, milk, blueberries and sugar. Cover and process until smooth. Add ice; cover and process until smooth. Pour into chilled glasses; serve immediately.

YIELD: 4 servings

FOUR-BERRY SMOOTHIES

Krista Johnson ● CROSSLAKE, MINNESOTA

"This smoothie tastes even more scrumptious when I think of how much money I save by whipping up my own at home. As a breakfast, it keeps me satisfied and full of energy all morning. My husband and I appreciate the fact that it's nutritious, refreshing and fast."

PREP/TOTAL TIME: 10 minutes

1-1/2	cups fat-free milk
1/2	cup frozen blackberries
1/2	cup frozen blueberries
1/2	cup frozen unsweetened raspberries
1/2	cup frozen unsweetened strawberries
2	tablespoons lemonade concentrate
1	tablespoon sugar
1/2	teaspoon vanilla extract

In a blender, combine all ingredients; cover and process until smooth. Pour into chilled glasses; serve immediately.

YIELD: 2 servings

LEMON ORANGE REFRESHER

Jodi Tuell ● RAYMOND, CALIFORNIA

"This cool, thirst-quenching beverage is in hot demand around my home. The tangy flavor of lemon and orange comes through sip after sip."

PREP/TOTAL TIME: 10 minutes

1	cup fat-free milk
1	carton (6 ounces) reduced-fat lemon yogurt
1	can (6 ounces) frozen unsweetened orange juice concentrate
1	tablespoon honey
1	teaspoon vanilla extract
1/4	teaspoon orange extract
15	ice cubes
5	long strips orange *or* lemon peel, twisted into spirals

In a blender, combine the first seven ingredients; cover and process until slushy. Pour into chilled glasses. Garnish with orange or lemon spirals. Serve immediately.

YIELD: 5 servings

SWEET FRUIT SMOOTHIES

Helen Reed ● AMHERST, OHIO

"Sipping one of these thick smoothies is a wonderful way to get fruit into your diet. They're a fun alternative to chocolate or vanilla milk shakes."

Prep/Total Time: 10 minutes

1	can (14 ounces) sweetened condensed milk
1	carton (8 ounces) strawberry yogurt
2	tablespoons lemon juice
1	can (8 ounces) crushed pineapple, undrained
1	medium ripe banana, sliced
1	cup halved fresh strawberries
1	cup crushed ice

In batches, process the milk, yogurt, lemon juice and fruit in a blender or food processor until smooth. Add ice; cover and process until smooth. Pour into chilled glasses; serve immediately.

YIELD: 5-6 servings

KIWI SMOOTHIES

Cindy Reams
PHILIPSBURG, PENNSYLVANIA

"These fresh-flavored smoothies can start a day out right or perk up an afternoon. My daughter created the recipe, and we all love it."

PREP/TOTAL TIME: 10 minutes

3	kiwifruit, peeled and cut into chunks
2	medium ripe bananas, cut into 4 pieces and frozen
1	cup frozen blueberries
1	cup (8 ounces) fat-free plain yogurt
3	tablespoons honey
1/4	teaspoon almond extract, optional
1-1/2	cups crushed ice

In a blender, combine the fruit, yogurt, honey and extract if desired; cover and process until combined. Add ice; cover and process until blended. Stir if necessary. Pour into chilled glasses; serve immediately.

YIELD: 4 servings

ORANGE PINEAPPLE SMOOTHIES

Sean Scales • WAUKESHA, WISCONSIN

"It's simple to whip up these smoothies since there's no fresh fruit to prepare. They're not too sweet or tart."

PREP/TOTAL TIME: 10 minutes

- 1 package (16 ounces) frozen pineapple chunks
- 1 cup orange juice concentrate
- 2 cans (5-1/2 ounces *each*) apricot nectar
- 2 cups ice cubes
- 1 envelope (.15 ounce) unsweetened orange soft drink mix

In a blender, combine half of the pineapple, orange juice concentrate, apricot nectar, ice cubes and soft drink mix; cover and process until smooth. Stir if necessary. Pour into chilled glasses. Repeat with remaining ingredients. Serve immediately.

YIELD: 6 servings

CHERRY BERRY SMOOTHIES

Macy Plummer • AVON, INDIANA

"You need just four ingredients to blend together these super-fast smoothies for breakfast. Or try whipping them up on a hot summer day for a cool and fruity treat."

PREP/TOTAL TIME: 5 minutes

- 1-1/2 cups unsweetened apple juice
- 1 cup frozen unsweetened raspberries
- 1 cup frozen pitted dark sweet cherries
- 1-1/2 cups raspberry sherbet

In a blender, combine the apple juice, raspberries and cherries. Add sherbet; cover and process until well blended. Pour into chilled glasses; serve immediately.

YIELD: 4 servings

OLD-FASHIONED STRAWBERRY SODA

Ginger Hubbard • ANDERSON, MISSOURI

"With just a quick pulse of the blender, you will have what I call a 'refreshing sipper,'—and you'll be asked for more!"

PREP/TOTAL TIME: 10 minutes

- 1 cup milk
- 1/2 cup fresh *or* frozen strawberries
- 1/2 cup vanilla ice cream, softened
- 2 tablespoons sugar
- 2 to 3 drops red food coloring, optional
- 1 cup ginger ale, chilled

In a blender, combine the milk, strawberries, ice cream, sugar and food coloring if desired; cover and process until smooth. Pour into two tall glasses. Add ginger ale and serve immediately.

YIELD: 2 servings

MANGO TANGO SMOOTHIES

Taste of Home Test Kitchen

"With a cup of milk and half cup of yogurt, this smoothie is rich in calcium and an excellent choice for breakfast on the run. For added convenience, you can buy mango chunks that are already peeled and chopped."

PREP/TOTAL TIME: 10 minutes

- 1 cup chopped peeled mango
- 1 medium ripe banana, frozen and sliced
- 1 cup fat-free milk
- 1/2 cup reduced-fat plain yogurt
- 1/2 cup unsweetened pineapple juice

In a blender, combine all ingredients; cover and process until smooth. Pour into chilled glasses; serve immediately.

YIELD: 2 servings

BERRY BANANA SMOOTHIES

Brenda Strohm • OMAHA, NEBRASKA

"I keep several bananas in the freezer so that I'm always ready to whip up this thick beverage for a quick breakfast or a tasty treat. Frozen fruit gives it a great consistency...it's like drinking a berry milk shake!"

PREP/TOTAL TIME: 10 minutes

- 1 cup reduced-fat vanilla yogurt
- 1 medium ripe banana, frozen and cut into chunks
- 1/4 cup *each* frozen unsweetened strawberries, blueberries, raspberries and blackberries
- 1 cup fat-free milk

In a blender, combine all the ingredients; cover and process until smooth. Pour into chilled glasses; serve immediately.

YIELD: 3 servings

FROTHY ORANGE DRINK

Sue Ellen Bumpus • LAMPASAS, TEXAS

"A teacher friend blended this sunny slush in a wink at school early one morning. It put a little zip in my day!"

PREP/TOTAL TIME: 10 minutes

- 1 can (6 ounces) frozen orange juice concentrate, unthawed
- 1 cup water
- 1 cup milk
- 1/2 cup sugar
- 1 teaspoon vanilla extract
- 8 to 10 ice cubes

In a blender, combine all ingredients; cover and process until thick and slushy. Pour into chilled glasses; serve immediately.

YIELD: 4 servings

STRAWBERRY BANANA SMOOTHIES

Linda Hendrix • MOUNDVILLE, MISSOURI

"If you're a fan of berries and bananas, you'll enjoy this frothy, delicious refresher. It's great to serve at breakfast or brunch. My young son comes running when he hears the blender going."

PREP/TOTAL TIME: 5 minutes

1 cup milk
1 cup water
1 package (10 ounces) frozen sweetened sliced strawberries, partially thawed
1 medium firm banana, cut into chunks
1 teaspoon vanilla extract
6 ice cubes

In a blender, combine all ingredients. Cover and process until smooth. Pour into chilled glasses; serve immediately.

YIELD: 4 servings

CHERRY CRANBERRY SHAKES

Gayle Lewis • YUCAIPA, CALIFORNIA

"We've enjoyed this frothy pink drink for many years. The combination of cranberry juice and cherry soda is tongue-tingling!"

PREP/TOTAL TIME: 10 minutes

1 cup cranberry juice, chilled
1 cup cherry soda, chilled
1 tablespoon milk *or* half-and-half cream
3/4 teaspoon vanilla extract
1 cup vanilla ice cream, softened

In a blender, combine all ingredients; cover and process until smooth. Pour into chilled glasses; serve immediately.

YIELD: 3 servings

MANDARIN BERRY COOLER

Nicole Harris • GREENBRIAR, PENNSYLVANIA

"It takes just a couple minutes to fix these fruity drinks. I especially like that they are just fruit, milk and ice—no added sugar."

PREP/TOTAL TIME: 5 minutes

1 can (11 ounces) mandarin oranges, drained
1 can (8 ounces) crushed pineapple, drained
1 cup sliced fresh strawberries
1 medium ripe banana, cut into chunks
6 ice cubes
3/4 cup milk

In a blender, combine the oranges, pineapple, strawberries and banana; cover and process until blended. Add ice and milk; cover and process until smooth. Pour into chilled glasses; serve immediately.

YIELD: 4 servings

CHAPTER 2
Ice Cream & Frozen Treats

Blueberry Cheesecake Ice Cream, 36

FROSTY FREEZER PIE

Sue Blow • LITITZ, PENNSYLVANIA

This pretty pie tastes so sweet and creamy, people will think you fussed. My family likes it best when it's made with orange sherbet.

PREP: 10 minutes + freezing

- 1 package (8 ounces) cream cheese, softened
- 1 jar (7 ounces) marshmallow creme
- 2 cups raspberry, orange *or* lime sherbet, softened
- 2 to 3 cups whipped topping
- 1 graham cracker crust (9 *or* 10 inches)

In a large mixing bowl, beat cream cheese and marshmallow creme until smooth. Stir in sherbet. Fold in whipped topping. Pour into crust. Freeze until firm. Remove from the freezer 10 minutes before serving. The pie may be frozen for up to 3 months.

YIELD: 8-10 servings

LEMON CUSTARD ICE CREAM

Susan Litwak • BELLEVUE, NEBRASKA

One thing I like about this ice cream—other than the pleasant lemon taste—is that it does not turn icy the next day.

PREP: 25 minutes + freezing

- 2 cups sugar
- 1/4 cup all-purpose flour
- 1/4 teaspoon salt
- 4 cups milk
- 4 eggs, lightly beaten
- 3 cups heavy whipping cream
- 1 cup lemon juice

In a large saucepan, combine the sugar, flour and salt. Gradually add milk. Bring to a boil over medium heat; cook and stir for 2 minutes or until thickened. Remove from the heat; cool slightly. Whisk a small amount of hot milk mixture into the eggs. Return all to the pan, whisking constantly. Cook and stir until mixture reaches 160° and coats the back of a metal spoon.

Remove from the heat. Cool quickly by placing pan in a bowl of ice water; stir for 2 minutes. Gently stir in the cream and lemon juice. Press plastic wrap onto surface of custard. Refrigerate for several hours or overnight.

Fill cylinder of ice cream freezer two-thirds full; freeze according to the manufacturer's directions. Refrigerate remaining mixture until ready to freeze. When ice cream is frozen, transfer to a freezer container; freeze for 2-4 hours before serving.

YIELD: 2 quarts (16 servings)

FRUITY SHERBET DESSERT

Rhonda Robertson • CASPER, WYOMING

Simple and refreshing, this dressed-up sherbet is a real treat in the heat of summer. With only four ingredients, it's a breeze to make.

PREP: 10 minutes + freezing

- 1/2 gallon pineapple sherbet, softened
- 2 packages (8 ounces *each*) frozen unsweetened raspberries, partially thawed
- 2 medium firm bananas, diced
- 1/2 teaspoon almond extract

Place sherbet in a large bowl. Fold in remaining ingredients. Cover and freeze for at least 3 hours or until firm.

YIELD: 2-1/2 quarts (20 servings)

BANANA SPLIT DESSERT

Mrs. Elmer Thorsheim ● RADCLIFFE, IOWA

"Here's a mouth-watering make-ahead dessert that looks scrumptious...and tastes as good as it looks!"

PREP: 30 minutes + freezing

3-1/2 cups graham cracker crumbs
2/3 cup butter, melted
4 to 5 medium bananas
1/2 gallon Neapolitan ice cream (block carton)
1 cup chopped walnuts
1 cup (6 ounces) chocolate chips
1/2 cup butter
2 cups confectioners' sugar
1 can (12 ounces) evaporated milk
1 teaspoon vanilla extract
1 pint heavy whipping cream

In a small bowl, combine crumbs and melted butter. Reserve 1/2 cup; press remaining crumbs into the bottom of a 15-in. x 11-in. x 2-in. baking dish. Slice bananas widthwise and layer over crust. Cut ice cream widthwise into eighths; place over bananas. Spread edges of ice cream slices to cover banana and form a smooth layer. Sprinkle with nuts. Cover and freeze until firm.

In a large saucepan, melt chocolate chips and butter; stir until smooth. Add sugar and milk. Cook, stirring constantly, over medium heat until slightly thickened and smooth. Remove from the heat; add vanilla. Cool. Pour over filling; freeze until firm.

In a large mixing bowl, whip cream until stiff peaks form; spread over chocolate layer. Top with reserved crumbs. Store in freezer (will keep for several weeks). Remove from freezer about 10 minutes before serving.

YIELD: 25 servings

APPLE PIE ICE CREAM

Robin Lamb ● RALEIGH, NORTH CAROLINA

"As a mother of a young family, I appreciate recipes that youngsters really enjoy. This apple-flavored ice cream is certainly one of them!"

PREP: 30 minutes + freezing

1-1/4 cups sugar
1/4 cup all-purpose flour
1/4 teaspoon salt
4 cups milk
4 eggs, lightly beaten
4 cups heavy whipping cream
3 tablespoons vanilla extract
1 can (21 ounces) apple pie filling, chopped
1 teaspoon ground cinnamon

In a large saucepan, combine the sugar, flour and salt; gradually stir in milk. Bring to a boil; cook and stir for 2 minutes or until thickened. Whisk a small amount of the hot mixture into the eggs. Return all to the pan, whisking constantly. Cook and stir over low heat until mixture reaches at least 160° and coats the back of a metal spoon.

Remove from the heat. Cool quickly by placing pan in a bowl of ice water; stir for 2 minutes. Stir in whipping cream and vanilla. Add pie filling and cinnamon. Press waxed paper onto surface of custard. Refrigerate for several hours or overnight.

Fill cylinder of ice cream freezer two-thirds full; freeze according to the manufacturer's directions. Refrigerate remaining mixture until ready to freeze. When ice cream is frozen, transfer to a freezer container; freeze for 2-4 hours before serving.

YIELD: 3 quarts (24 servings)

FROZEN CHOCOLATE CRUNCH

Flo Burtnett • GAGE, OKLAHOMA

"An original recipe of mine, this cool and crunchy concoction has won prizes in a couple of recipe contests. Everyone agrees the fun mix of chocolate, crushed cookies, whipping cream and nuts makes a tempting alternative to ice cream."

PREP: 1 hour 30 minutes + freezing

8   squares (1 ounce *each*) German sweet chocolate, chopped
2/3   cup light corn syrup
2   cups heavy whipping cream, *divided*
1-1/2   cups coarsely crushed cream-filled chocolate sandwich cookies (about 12 cookies)
1   cup chopped walnuts
Additional chopped walnuts and crushed cream-filled chocolate sandwich cookies, optional

In a heavy saucepan, melt chocolate and corn syrup; stir until smooth. Stir in 1/2 cup cream. Refrigerate for 1 hour or until cool. Stir in crushed cookies and walnuts. In a small mixing bowl, beat remaining cream until stiff peaks form; fold into chocolate mixture.

Spread into a 9-in. square dish. Cover and freeze for 4-6 hours or until firm. Sprinkle with additional walnuts and crushed cookies if desired.

YIELD: 12-16 servings

LEMON LIME DESSERT

Marsha Schindler • FORT WAYNE, INDIANA

"This make-ahead treat offers a wonderfully refreshing blend of citrus flavors. Topped with a smooth lemon sauce, it's the perfect ending to any meal. Using an electric mixer makes it easy to combine the lime sherbet and vanilla ice cream."

PREP: 20 minutes COOK: 10 minutes + freezing

1-1/2   cups graham cracker crumbs (about 24 squares)
14   tablespoons butter, melted, *divided*
1-1/4   cups sugar, *divided*
1/2   gallon vanilla ice cream, softened
1   quart lime sherbet, softened
2   eggs, lightly beaten
1/4   cup lemon juice

In a large bowl, combine the cracker crumbs, 7 tablespoons butter and 1/4 cup sugar. Press into an ungreased 13-in. x 9-in. x 2-in. dish; freeze until firm. In a large mixing bowl, combine ice cream and sherbet; pour over the crust. Freeze until firm.

In a heavy saucepan, combine the eggs and remaining sugar. Stir in the lemon juice and remaining butter. Cook and stir until mixture reaches 160° and coats the back of a metal spoon. Cover and refrigerate until cool.

Spread over ice cream mixture. Cover and freeze for 3 hours or overnight. May be frozen for up to 2 months. Just before serving, remove from the freezer and cut into squares.

YIELD: 12-15 servings

Softening Ice Cream

Ice cream is often softened for recipes. To soften it in the refrigerator, transfer from the freezer to the fridge 20-30 minutes before using. Or let it stand at room temperature for 10-15 minutes.

BLUEBERRY CHEESECAKE ICE CREAM

Melissa Symington • NECHE, NORTH DAKOTA

"After sampling this flavor at an ice cream stand, I kept trying to duplicate it at home until it was just right."

PREP: 25 minutes + freezing BAKE: 10 minutes + cooling

- 1/2 **cup sugar**
- 1 **tablespoon cornstarch**
- 1/2 **cup water**
- 1-1/4 **cups fresh *or* frozen blueberries**
- 1 **tablespoon lemon juice**

GRAHAM CRACKER MIXTURE:
- 2-1/4 **cups graham cracker crumbs (about 36 squares)**
- 2 **tablespoons sugar**
- 1/2 **teaspoon ground cinnamon**
- 1/2 **cup butter, melted**

ICE CREAM:
- 1-1/2 **cups sugar**
- 1 **package (3.4 ounces) instant cheesecake *or* vanilla pudding mix**
- 1 **quart heavy whipping cream**
- 2 **cups milk**
- 2 **teaspoons vanilla extract**

In a small saucepan, combine sugar and cornstarch. Gradually stir in water until smooth. Stir in blueberries and lemon juice. Bring to a boil. Reduce heat; simmer, uncovered, for 5 minutes or until slightly thickened, stirring occasionally. Cover and refrigerate until chilled.

In a large bowl, combine the cracker crumbs, sugar and cinnamon. Stir in butter. Pat into an ungreased 15-in. x 10-in. x 1-in. baking pan. Bake at 350° for 10-15 minutes or until lightly browned. Cool completely on a wire rack.

Meanwhile, in a large bowl, whisk the ice cream ingredients. Fill ice cream freezer cylinder two-thirds full; freeze according to manufacturer's directions. Refrigerate remaining mixture until ready to freeze. Whisk before adding to ice cream freezer (mixture will have some lumps).

Crumble the graham cracker mixture. In a large container, layer the ice cream, graham cracker mixture and blueberry sauce three times; swirl. Freeze.

YIELD: 2 quarts (16 servings)

BUTTER PECAN ICE CREAM

Jenny White • GLEN, MISSISSIPPI

"This rich, buttery ice cream sure beats store-bought versions. And with its pretty color and plentiful pecan crunch, it's nice enough to serve guests."

PREP: 15 minutes + freezing

- 1/2 **cup chopped pecans**
- 1 **tablespoon butter**
- 1-1/2 **cups half-and-half cream**
- 1 **cup packed brown sugar**
- 2 **eggs, lightly beaten**
- 1/2 **cup heavy whipping cream**
- 1 **teaspoon vanilla extract**

In a small skillet, toast pecans in butter for 5-6 minutes or until lightly browned. Cool.

In a heavy saucepan, heat half-and-half to 175°; stir in the brown sugar until dissolved. Whisk a small amount of hot cream mixture into the eggs; return all to the pan, whisking constantly. Cook and stir over low heat until mixture reaches at least 160° and coats the back of a metal spoon.

Remove from the heat. Cool quickly by placing pan in a bowl of ice water; stir for 2 minutes. Stir in whipping cream and vanilla. Press plastic wrap onto the surface of custard. Refrigerate for several hours or overnight. Stir in toasted pecans.

Fill cylinder of ice cream freezer two-thirds full; freeze according to the manufacturer's directions. Refrigerate remaining mixture until ready to freeze. Allow to ripen in ice cream freezer or firm up in the refrigerator freezer for 2-4 hours before serving.

YIELD: 1 quart (8 servings)

CHOCOLATE MALTED ICE CREAM

Rose Hare
MOUNTAIN HOME, IDAHO

"As a child, I helped crank out gallons of homemade ice cream. Thanks to this recipe, I'm carrying on the tradition."

PREP: 15 minutes
COOK: 10 minutes + freezing

- 2 **cups milk**
- 1 **cup sugar**
- 1/2 **cup chocolate malted milk powder**
- 5 **eggs, lightly beaten**
- 4 **cups heavy whipping cream**
- 1 **cup malted milk balls, coarsely crushed**
- 1 **tablespoon vanilla extract**

In a large saucepan, heat milk to 175°; stir in sugar and malted milk powder until dissolved. Whisk a small amount of the hot mixture into the eggs. Return all to the pan, whisking constantly. Cook and stir over low heat until mixture reaches at least 160° and coats the back of a metal spoon.

Remove from the heat. Cool quickly by placing pan in a bowl of ice water; stir for 2 minutes. Stir in the whipping cream, malted milk balls and vanilla. Press waxed paper onto surface of custard. Refrigerate for several hours or overnight.

Fill cylinder of ice cream freezer two-thirds full; freeze according to the manufacturer's directions. Refrigerate remaining mixture until ready to freeze. When ice cream is frozen, transfer to a freezer container; freeze for 2-4 hours before serving.

YIELD: 2 quarts (16 servings)

CHOCOLATE RASPBERRY DESSERT

Judy Schut ● GRAND RAPIDS, MICHIGAN

"Guests find wedges of this fruity frozen pie irresistible. The crustless concoction has a creamy mousse-like consistency that's melt-in-your-mouth good."

PREP: 10 minutes + freezing

1 cup 1% cottage cheese
3/4 cup fat-free milk
1/3 cup raspberry spreadable fruit
1 package (1.4 ounces) sugar-free instant chocolate pudding mix
1 carton (8 ounces) frozen reduced-fat whipped topping, thawed
1 square (1 ounce) semisweet chocolate, melted
1/2 cup frozen unsweetened raspberries, thawed

In a blender, combine the cottage cheese, milk and spreadable fruit; cover and process until smooth. Add pudding mix; cover and process until smooth. Pour into a large bowl; fold in whipped topping. Spoon into a 9-in. pie plate. Drizzle with chocolate. Cover and freeze for 8 hours or overnight.

Let stand at room temperature for 20 minutes before serving. Garnish with raspberries.

YIELD: 8 servings

THREE-FRUIT FROZEN YOGURT

Wendy Hilton ● LAUREL, MISSISSIPPI

"This recipe takes just minutes to combine the bananas, strawberries and pineapple with a few other ingredients before popping everything in the freezer."

PREP: 15 minutes + freezing

2 medium ripe bananas
1 package (10 ounces) frozen sweetened sliced strawberries, thawed and drained
1 can (8 ounces) crushed pineapple, drained
1 carton (6 ounces) strawberry yogurt
1/2 cup sugar
1 carton (8 ounces) frozen whipped topping, thawed

In a large bowl, mash the bananas and strawberries. Stir in the pineapple, yogurt and sugar. Fold in the whipped topping. Cover and freezer until firm. May be frozen for up to 1 month.

YIELD: 1-1/2 quarts (12 servings)

MACAROON ICE CREAM TORTE

Barbara Carlucci ● ORANGE PARK, FLORIDA

"I often make this recipe for special occasions. I found it in a ladies' club cookbook where it was called The Girdlebuster."

PREP: 15 minutes + freezing

24 macaroon cookies, crumbled
1 quart coffee ice cream, softened
1 quart chocolate ice cream, softened
1 cup milk chocolate toffee bits
  or 4 (1.4 ounces) Heath candy bars, coarsely chopped
Hot fudge topping, warmed

Sprinkle a third of the cookies into an ungreased 9-in. springform pan. Top with 2 cups coffee ice cream, a third of the cookies, 2 cups chocolate ice cream and 1/2 cup toffee bits. Repeat layers. Cover and freeze until firm. May be frozen for up to 2 months.

Remove from the freezer 10 minutes before serving. Remove sides of pan. Cut into wedges; drizzle with hot fudge topping.

YIELD: 12-16 servings

STRAWBERRY CHEESECAKE ICE CREAM

Irene Yoder • FILLMORE, NEW YORK

"This custard-like ice cream is so rich and creamy that it tastes like you fussed for hours. But it's easy to make...and pretty, too. I like to serve it with chocolate fudge sauce."

PREP: 20 minutes + freezing

- 3 **cups sugar**
- 3 **tablespoons all-purpose flour**

Pinch salt

- 8 **cups milk**
- 4 **eggs, lightly beaten**
- 1 **package (8 ounces) cream cheese, cubed**
- 1 **teaspoon vanilla extract**
- 3 **cups fresh *or* frozen unsweetened strawberries, thawed**
- 2 **cups heavy whipping cream**

In a heavy saucepan, combine the sugar, flour and salt. Gradually add milk until smooth. Bring to a boil over medium heat; cook and stir for 2 minutes or until thickened. Remove from the heat; cool slightly.

Whisk a small amount of hot milk mixture into the eggs; return all to the pan, whisking constantly. Cook and stir over low heat until mixture reaches at least 160° and coats the back of a metal spoon. Stir in the cream cheese until melted.

Remove from the heat. Cool quickly by placing pan in a bowl of ice water; stir for 2 minutes. Stir in vanilla. Press plastic wrap onto surface of custard. Refrigerate for several hours or overnight.

Stir strawberries and cream into custard. Fill cylinder of ice cream freezer two-thirds full; freeze according to the manufacturer's directions. Refrigerate remaining mixture until ready to freeze. When ice cream is frozen, transfer to a freezer container; freeze for 2-4 hours before serving.

YIELD: 1 gallon (32 servings)

ROCKY ROAD ICE CREAM

Dale Langford • ATWATER, CALIFORNIA

"My daughters always want to put this ice cream in cones just like the ice cream shops do. We especially like the marshmallows, chocolate chips and chopped pecans. Sometimes we even add extra chips on top...and whipped cream, too."

PREP: 15 minutes + freezing

- 3 **cups milk**
- 3 **cups half-and-half cream**
- 9 **squares (1 ounce *each*) semisweet chocolate**
- 2-3/4 **cups sugar**
- 3/4 **teaspoon salt**
- 6 **cups heavy whipping cream**
- 3 **cups miniature marshmallows**
- 2-1/4 **cups miniature semisweet chocolate chips**
- 1-1/2 **cups chopped pecans**
- 6 **teaspoons vanilla extract**

In a large saucepan, combine milk and half-and-half; heat to 175°. Add chocolate, sugar and salt; stir until chocolate is melted and sugar is dissolved.

Remove from the heat. Cool quickly by placing pan in a bowl of ice water; stir for 2 minutes. Cool completely. Transfer to a large bowl; stir in the remaining ingredients. Cover and refrigerate for 30 minutes.

Fill cylinder of ice cream freezer two-thirds full; freeze according to the manufacturer's directions. Refrigerate remaining mixture until ready to freeze. When ice cream is frozen, transfer to a freezer container; freeze for 2-4 hours before serving.

YIELD: about 4-1/2 quarts (36 servings)

GRAPE SHERBET

Sherry Rominger
ROGERS, ARKANSAS

"My husband, two daughters and I first enjoyed this refreshing treat at our friends' house. They graciously shared the recipe after we all raved about it. The sherbet is always popular at ice cream socials."

PREP: 5 minutes + freezing

1-3/4	cups grape juice
3	tablespoons lemon juice
1/2	cup sugar
1-3/4	cups half-and half cream

In a large bowl, combine all the ingredients. Fill cylinder of ice cream freezer; freeze according to manufacturer's directions. Transfer sherbet to a container; cover and freeze for 4 hours or until firm.

YIELD: 1 quart (8 servings)

BLACKBERRY FROZEN YOGURT

Rebecca Baird ● Salt Lake City, Utah

"I pair sweet blackberries with tangy vanilla yogurt to churn out this purple delight. You could also use boysenberries, raspberries or strawberries."

Prep: 30 minutes + freezing

- 5 cups fresh *or* frozen blackberries
- 1/3 cup water
- 2 tablespoons lemon juice
- 1 cup sugar
- 2 teaspoons vanilla extract
- 4 cups (32 ounces) fat-free frozen vanilla yogurt

In a food processor, puree blackberries, water and lemon juice. Strain blackberries, reserving juice and pulp. Discard seeds. Return pureed blackberries to food processor; add sugar and vanilla. Cover and process until smooth.

In a large bowl, combine yogurt and blackberry mixture. Fill cylinder of ice cream freezer two-thirds full; freeze according to the manufacturer's directions. Refrigerate remaining mixture until ready to freeze. When yogurt is frozen, transfer to a freezer container; freeze for 2-4 hours before serving.

Yield: 8 servings

REFRESHING ORANGE ICE

Carol Lydon ● Philadelphia, Pennsylvania

"This sherbet has been part of my family's Thanksgiving tradition for generations. The tangy, creamy flavor complements the turkey and all the trimmings."

Prep: 10 minutes + freezing

- 3 cups water, *divided*
- 1 cup sugar
- 1 can (12 ounces) frozen orange juice concentrate, thawed
- 2 tablespoons lemon juice
- 1/2 cup half-and-half cream

In a saucepan, bring 1 cup water and sugar to a boil, stirring frequently. Boil for 1 minute or until sugar is dissolved. Remove from the heat; stir in orange juice concentrate, lemon juice and remaining water. Transfer to a freezer-proof mixing bowl. Cover and freeze until firm.

Remove from the freezer. Beat until blended. Beat in cream. Cover and return to freezer. Remove from the freezer 20 minutes before serving.

Yield: 10-12 servings

MANGO LEMON SORBET

Taste of Home Test Kitchen

"You'll love the sunny color and fruity flavor of this light dessert. If you can't find mangoes, substitute fresh peaches."

Prep: 5 minutes + freezing

- 1/2 cup cold water
- 3 cups chopped peeled mangoes *or* fresh peaches (about 2 pounds)
- 1 cup sugar
- 2 tablespoons lemon juice

In a blender, combine water and mangoes; cover and process until smooth. Add sugar and lemon juice; cover and process until sugar is dissolved, about 1 minute.

Fill cylinder of ice cream freezer; freeze according to manufacturer's directions. Transfer sorbet to a container; cover and freeze for 4 hours or until firm.

Yield: 6 servings

PINEAPPLE ORANGE SHERBET

Angela Oelschlaeger • TONGANOXIE, KANSAS

"What better way to end a meal than on a sweet note? This delightful sherbet is low in fat but high in demand."

PREP: 15 minutes + freezing

3   **cans (12 ounces** *each***) orange soda**
2   **cans (8 ounces** *each***) unsweetened crushed pineapple, undrained**
1-1/2   **cups sugar**
1   **can (12 ounces) fat-free evaporated milk**
1/8   **teaspoon salt**

In a large bowl, combine all ingredients. Fill ice cream freezer cylinder two-thirds full; freeze according to manufacturer's directions (refrigerate remaining mixture until ready to freeze).

Transfer to a freezer container; allow sherbet to firm up in the refrigerator freezer for 2-4 hours before serving.

YIELD: about 2 quarts (12 servings)

RASPBERRY ICE CREAM

Diana Leskauskas • KNOXVILLE, TENNESSEE

"When our garden produces an abundance of raspberries, we know it's time to make this fruity frozen dessert. It's super in the summertime."

PREP: 10 minutes + freezing

2   **cups fresh** *or* **frozen raspberries**
1   **cup half-and-half cream**
1   **cup sugar**
2   **cups heavy whipping cream**
2   **teaspoons vanilla extract**

Place the raspberries in a blender; cover and process on medium-high speed until chopped; set aside. In a large saucepan, heat half-and-half to 175°; stir in sugar until dissolved. Remove from the heat. Stir in whipping cream and vanilla. Fold in raspberries. Refrigerate until chilled.

Fill cylinder of ice cream freezer two-thirds full; freeze according to the manufacturer's directions. Refrigerate remaining mixture until ready to freeze. When ice cream is frozen, transfer to a freezer container; freeze for 2-4 hours before serving.

YIELD: about 1-1/2 quarts (12 servings)

PUMPKIN ICE CREAM PIE

Suzanne Mckinley • LYONS, GEORGIA

"Although it looks like you fussed, this pretty layered pie is easy to assemble with convenient canned pumpkin, store-bought candy bars and a prepared crust."

PREP: 10 minutes + freezing

3   **Heath candy bars (1.4 ounces** *each***), crushed,** *divided*
3   **cups vanilla ice cream, softened,** *divided*
1   **chocolate crumb crust (9 inches)**
1/2   **cup canned pumpkin**
2   **tablespoons sugar**
1/2   **teaspoon ground cinnamon**
1/4   **teaspoon ground nutmeg**

Combine two-thirds of the crushed candy bars and 2 cups ice cream.

Spoon into crust; freeze for 1 hour or until firm.

In a large bowl, combine the pumpkin, sugar, cinnamon, nutmeg and remaining ice cream. Spoon over ice cream layer in crust. Sprinkle with remaining crushed candy bars. Cover and freeze for 8 hours or up to 2 months. Remove from the freezer 10-15 minutes before serving.

YIELD: 8 servings

COCONUT CREAM DESSERT

Carol Beamer • GLENVILLE, WEST VIRGINIA

"Butter-flavored crackers make the crunchy crust for this frozen take on coconut cream pie. Try sprinkling chopped nuts on top instead of the coconut."

PREP: 15 minutes + freezing

2-1/2   cups crushed butter-flavored crackers (about 68 crackers)
1/2   cup plus 2 tablespoons butter, melted
1/2   gallon vanilla ice cream, softened
1/2   cup cold milk
2   packages (3.4 ounces *each*) instant coconut cream pudding mix
1   carton (8 ounces) frozen whipped topping, thawed
1/3   cup flaked coconut, toasted

In a small bowl, combine the cracker crumbs and butter. Press into an ungreased 13-in. x 9-in. x 2-in. dish.

In a large mixing bowl, combine the ice cream, milk and pudding mixes until blended. Spread over the crust; top with whipped topping and coconut. Cover and freeze for up to 2 months. Remove from the freezer 15 minutes before serving.

YIELD: 12-15 servings

CRANBERRY VELVET FREEZE

Pat Seville • HAGERSTOWN, MARYLAND

"Everyone in my family loves this dessert. I normally serve it at Thanksgiving and Christmas when we're all together."

PREP: 10 minutes + freezing

2   cans (16 ounces *each*) whole-berry cranberry sauce
2   cans (one 20 ounces, one 8 ounces) crushed pineapple, drained
1   package (10-1/2 ounces) miniature marshmallows
1   cup green maraschino cherries, quartered
1   cup red maraschino cherries, quartered
1   teaspoon lemon juice

3   cups heavy whipping cream, whipped

In a large bowl, combine the cranberry sauce, pineapple, marshmallows, cherries and lemon juice. Fold in whipped cream. Spoon into an ungreased 13-in. x 9-in. x 2-in. dish. Cover and freeze overnight. Remove from the freezer 10 minutes before serving.

YIELD: 12-16 servings

CREAMY LIME SHERBET

Mary Beth Dell Spiess • INDUSTRY, TEXAS

"The lime flavor in this cool treat is perfect, and the pastel color is so pretty."

PREP: 15 minutes + freezing

1   package (3 ounces) lime gelatin
1   cup boiling water
1-1/4   cups sugar
1   can (6 ounces) frozen limeade concentrate, thawed
Dash salt
4   cups milk
2   cups half-and-half cream
8   drops green food coloring, optional

In a large bowl, dissolve gelatin in water. Stir in the sugar, limeade and salt until sugar is dissolved. Add remaining ingredients.

Fill cylinder of ice cream freezer two-thirds full; freeze according to the manufacturer's directions. Refrigerate remaining mixture until ready to freeze. When sherbet is frozen, transfer to a freezer container; freeze for 2-4 hours before serving.

YIELD: about 2 quarts (16 servings)

APPLE PIE A LA MODE

Trisha Kruse ● EAGLE, IDAHO

"Here is a family favorite that combines apple pie filling and butter pecan ice cream with caramel topping and chopped nuts. I created it when trying to think up a rich dessert to complete a dinner party menu."

PREP: 20 minutes + freezing

1   can (21 ounces) apple pie filling
1   graham cracker crust (9 inches)
2   cups butter pecan ice cream, softened
1   jar (12 ounces) caramel ice cream topping
1/4   cup chopped pecans, toasted

Spread half the pie filling over crust. Top with half the ice cream; cover and freeze for 30 minutes. Drizzle with half the caramel topping; cover and freeze for 30 minutes. Top with remaining pie filling; cover and freeze for 30 minutes. Top with remaining ice cream; cover and freeze until firm. May be frozen for up to 2 months.

Remove from the freezer about 30 minutes before serving. Warm remaining caramel topping; drizzle some on serving plates. Top with a slice of pie; drizzle remaining caramel topping over pie and sprinkle with pecans.

YIELD: 6-8 servings

PEACH FROZEN YOGURT

Stephanie Nohr ● CORNELL, WISCONSIN

"When peaches are in season, we order them by the bushel. This quick and creamy frozen treat has wonderful fresh fruit flavor. It's a big hit with everyone in my family."

PREP: 15 minutes + freezing

2   cups fresh *or* frozen unsweetened sliced peaches, thawed
1   envelope unflavored gelatin
1/4   cup cold water
1/4   cup sugar
2   cups (16 ounces) reduced-fat vanilla yogurt

Place the peaches in a blender; cover and process until pureed. Set aside. In a small saucepan, sprinkle gelatin over cold water; let stand for 1 minute. Stir in sugar. Cook and stir over low heat until gelatin and sugar are dissolved.

In a large bowl, combine the yogurt, peach puree and gelatin mixture until blended. Pour into an ungreased 9-in. square dish. Cover and freeze for 3-4 hours or until partially set.

Cut into pieces and place in a large mixing bowl; beat on medium speed until smooth. Transfer to a freezer container. Cover and freeze until firm, about 2 hours.

YIELD: 6 servings

Scoop Ice Cream Swiftly

When scooping ice cream, do so quickly and return the unused portion to freezer as soon as possible. Thawing and refreezing causes ice crystals to form on the ice cream's surface.

CANTALOUPE SHERBET

Mary Dixson
DECATUR, ALABAMA

Melon lovers are sure to enjoy this frosty dessert.

PREP: 20 minutes + freezing

1	small ripe cantaloupe
2	cups cold fat-free milk, *divided*
1/3	cup sugar
1	envelope unflavored gelatin
1/4	cup light corn syrup
1/4	teaspoon salt

Cut cantaloupe in half; discard seeds. Scoop out pulp (there should be about 4 cups melon). Place cantaloupe and 1 cup milk in a blender or food processor; cover and process until smooth.

In a large saucepan, combine sugar and remaining milk. Sprinkle gelatin over top; let stand for 1 minute. Heat over low heat, stirring until gelatin is complete dissolved. Stir in the corn syrup, salt and pureed cantaloupe. Pour into a 13-in. x 9-in. x 2-in. pan. Cover and freeze until partially frozen, about 3 hours, stirring occasionally.

Place cantaloupe mixture in a blender; cover and process until smooth. Return to the pan. Cover and freeze until almost frozen, about 1 hour.

YIELD: 6 servings

FROZEN MUD PIE

Debbie Terenzini ● LUSBY, MARYLAND

"*Here's one of those 'looks like you fussed' desserts that is so easy it's become a standard for me. The cookie crust is a snap to make.*"

PREP: 40 minutes + freezing

1-1/2   cups cream-filled chocolate sandwich cookie crumbs
1-1/2   teaspoons sugar, optional
1/4   cup butter, melted
4   cups chocolate chip *or* coffee ice cream, softened
1/4   cup chocolate syrup, *divided*
Additional cream-filled chocolate sandwich cookies, optional

In a small bowl, combine cookie crumbs and sugar if desired. Stir in butter. Press onto the bottom and up the sides of an ungreased 9-in. pie plate. Refrigerate for 30 minutes.

Spoon 2 cups ice cream into crust. Drizzle with half the chocolate syrup; swirl with knife. Carefully top with remaining ice cream. Drizzle with remaining syrup; swirl with a knife. Cover and freeze until firm.

Remove from the freezer 10-15 minutes before serving. Garnish with whole cookies if desired.

YIELD: 8 servings

FESTIVE MINT CREAM DESSERT

Sally Hook ● MONTGOMERY, TEXAS

"*Mint ice cream and colorful sprinkles make this cool concoction perfect for holiday parties or meals. For a chocolaty dessert, use rocky road or chocolate ice cream instead.*"

PREP: 25 minutes + freezing

3/4   cup butter, *divided*
1   package (16 ounces) chocolate cream-filled sandwich cookies, crushed
8   cups mint chocolate chip ice cream, softened
1-1/2   cups milk chocolate chips
1   cup confectioners' sugar
3/4   cup evaporated milk
1   carton (16 ounces) frozen whipped topping, thawed
Chocolate syrup and red and green sprinkles, optional

In a microwave, melt 1/2 cup butter. Stir in cookie crumbs. Press into a 13-in. x 9-in. x 2-in. dish. Freeze for 30 minutes or until firm. Spread ice cream over crust; return to the freezer until firm.

In a large saucepan, combine chocolate chips, confectioners' sugar, milk and remaining butter. Bring to a boil, stirring frequently. Cook and stir for 3-5 minutes or until thickened. Cool to room temperature. When cool, spread over ice cream; return to freezer until firm.

Spread whipped topping over ice cream (dish will be full). Cover and freeze until firm. Remove from the freezer 15-20 minutes before serving. If desired, drizzle with chocolate syrup and top with sprinkles.

YIELD: 24 servings

PEPPERMINT ICE CREAM

Berneice Metcalf • LEAVENWORTH, WASHINGTON

"With flecks of peppermint candy, this ice cream is perfect for the holidays, but we enjoy scoops of it year-round."

PREP: 15 minutes + freezing

- 1-1/2 cups half-and-half cream
- 3/4 cup sugar
- 1/4 teaspoon salt
- 4 egg yolks
- 2 cups heavy whipping cream
- 4-1/2 to 6 teaspoons vanilla extract
- 1 to 1-1/4 cups crushed peppermint candy

In a large saucepan, heat half-and-half to 175°; stir in sugar and salt until dissolved. Whisk a small amount of the hot mixture into the eggs. Return all to the pan, whisking constantly. Cook and stir over low heat until mixture reaches at least 160° and coats the back of a metal spoon.

Remove from the heat. Cool quickly by placing pan in a bowl of ice water; stir for 2 minutes. Stir in whipping cream and vanilla. Press plastic wrap onto surface of custard. Refrigerate for several hours or overnight.

Fill cylinder of ice cream freezer two-thirds full; freeze according to the manufacturer's directions. Refrigerate remaining mixture until ready to freeze. When ice cream is frozen, transfer to a freezer container; stir in peppermint candy. Freeze for 2-4 hours before serving.

YIELD: 1 quart (8 servings)

TRIPLE SHERBET TREAT

Mrs. Howard Hinseth • MINNEAPOLIS, MINNESOTA

"For a special, refreshing and lovely treat, try this sherbet dessert. Our children requested it many times over the years."

PREP: 15 minutes + freezing

- 1 package (14-1/2 ounces) coconut macaroon cookies, crumbled
- 1 carton (12 ounces) frozen whipped topping, thawed
- 1/2 cup chopped pecans, optional
- 1/2 cup flaked coconut
- 1 pint *each* orange, lemon and lime sherbet, softened

In a large bowl, combine the cookie crumbs, whipped topping, pecans and coconut. Spread half into a 13-in. x 9-in. x 2-in. dish. Spread with orange sherbet; freeze for 10-15 minutes. Repeat with lemon and lime layers. Top with remaining cookie mixture. Cover and freeze until firm.

YIELD: 12-16 servings

CRUNCHY ICE CREAM DESSERT

Mildred Sherrer • FORT WORTH, TEXAS

"I like to start my meal prep with dessert. I sandwich vanilla ice cream with layers of cereal, peanuts and coconut. Then freeze until ready to serve."

PREP: 25 minutes + freezing

- 2 cups crushed Rice Chex
- 2/3 cup packed brown sugar
- 1/2 cup chopped peanuts
- 1/2 cup flaked coconut
- 1/2 cup butter, melted
- 1/2 gallon vanilla ice cream

In a large bowl, combine the cereal, brown sugar, peanuts and coconut.

Drizzle with butter; stir until combined. Press half of the mixture into an ungreased 13-in. x 9-in. x 2-in. dish. Cut ice cream into 3/4-in.-thick slices; arrange evenly over crust. Top with remaining crumb mixture; press down lightly. Cover and freeze until serving.

YIELD: 12-15 servings

CHERRY NUT ICE CREAM

Mary Lou Patrick
EAST WENATCHEE, WASHINGTON

"Since my husband is a cherry grower, I had our grandsons help me develop this ice cream recipe that used the fruit."

PREP: 15 minutes + freezing

- 6 cups heavy whipping cream
- 1 cup sugar
- 1/8 teaspoon salt
- 3 egg yolks
- 3 teaspoons almond extract
- 2 cups fresh *or* frozen pitted dark sweet cherries, thawed and cut into quarters
- 1 cup flaked coconut, toasted
- 1 cup sliced almonds, toasted
- 1 milk chocolate candy bar (7 ounces), chopped

In a saucepan, heat cream over medium heat until bubbles form around sides of saucepan; stir in sugar and salt until dissolved. Whisk a small amount of the cream into the eggs. Return all to the pan, whisking constantly. Cook and stir over low heat until mixture reaches 160° and coats the back of a metal spoon.

Remove from heat. Stir in extract. Cool by placing pan in a bowl of ice water; stir for 2 minutes. Press waxed paper onto surface of custard. Refrigerate several hours or overnight.

Fill cylinder of ice cream freezer two-thirds full; freeze according to the manufacturer's directions. Refrigerate remaining mixture until ready to freeze. Stir the cherries, coconut, almonds and chocolate into the ice cream just until combined. Transfer to a freezer container; freeze for 2-4 hours before serving.

YIELD: 1-1/2 quarts (12 servings)

MINT CHOCOLATE CHIP PIE

Dolores Scofield • WEST SHOKAN, NEW YORK

"You'll need only three ingredients to fix this refreshing make-ahead dessert that features a cool combination of mint and chocolate."

PREP: 10 minutes + freezing

- 6 to 8 cups mint chocolate chip ice cream, softened
- 1 chocolate crumb crust (9 inches)
- 2 squares (1 ounce *each*) semisweet chocolate

Spoon ice cream into crust. In a microwave-safe bowl, melt chocolate; stir until smooth. Drizzle over ice cream. Freeze for 6-8 hours or overnight. Remove from the freezer 15 minutes before serving. Pie may be frozen for up to 2 months.

YIELD: 6-8 servings

GEORGIA PEACH ICE CREAM

Marguerite Ethridge • AMERICUS, GEORGIA

"My state is well known for growing good peaches. This delicious recipe has been a favorite for almost 50 years."

PREP: 20 minutes COOK: 15 minutes + freezing

- 1 quart milk
- 2-1/4 cups sugar, *divided*
- 1/2 teaspoon salt
- 4 eggs, lightly beaten
- 2 cans (14 ounces *each*) sweetened condensed milk
- 1-3/4 pounds fresh peaches, peeled and sliced

In a large heavy saucepan, heat milk to 175°; stir in 1 cup sugar and salt until dissolved. Whisk a small amount of the hot mixture into the eggs. Return all to the pan, whisking constantly. Cook and stir over low heat until mixture reaches at least 160° and coats the back of a metal spoon.

Remove from the heat. Cool quickly by placing pan in a bowl of ice water; stir for 2 minutes. Stir in sweetened condensed milk. Press plastic wrap onto surface of custard. Refrigerate for several hours or overnight.

When ready to freeze, mash peaches with remaining sugar in a small bowl; let stand for 30 minutes. Combine milk mixture and peaches in an ice cream freezer. Freeze according to manufacturer's directions.

YIELD: 3-3/4 quarts

ICE CREAM SANDWICH DESSERT

Jody Koerber • CALEDONIA, WISCONSIN

"No one will believe this awesome dessert is just dressed-up ice cream sandwiches."

PREP: 15 minutes + freezing

- 19 ice cream sandwiches
- 1 carton (12 ounces) frozen whipped topping, thawed
- 1 jar (11-3/4 ounces) hot fudge ice cream topping
- 1 cup salted peanuts

Cut one ice cream sandwich in half. Place one whole and one half sandwich along a short side of an ungreased 13-in. x 9-in. x 2-in. pan. Arrange eight sandwiches in opposite direction in the pan. Spread with half of the whipped topping. Spoon fudge topping by teaspoonfuls onto whipped topping. Sprinkle with 1/2 cup peanuts. Repeat layers with remaining ice cream sandwiches, whipped topping and peanuts (pan will be full).

Cover and freeze for up to 2 months. Remove from freezer 20 minutes before serving.

YIELD: 12-15 servings

PEANUT BUTTER ICE CREAM

Sigrid Guillot ● THIBODAUX, LOUISIANA

"It's the big flock of ducks my husband and I used to raise that inspired me to create this recipe. When we found ourselves with a surplus of their eggs, ice cream seemed a good place to put them."

PREP: 15 minutes COOK: 15 minutes + freezing

1	envelope unflavored gelatin
1/4	cup cold water
1-3/4	cups milk
1	cup sugar
1/4	teaspoon salt
3	egg yolks
3	packages (16 ounces *each*) peanut butter cups, crumbled
2	cups evaporated milk
1	tablespoon vanilla extract

In a small saucepan, sprinkle gelatin over cold water; let stand for 1 minute. Heat over low heat, stirring until gelatin is completely dissolved; set aside.

In a large saucepan, heat milk to 175°; stir in sugar and salt until dissolved. Whisk a small amount of the hot mixture into the eggs. Return all to the pan, whisking constantly.

Cook and stir over low heat until mixture reaches at least 160° and coats the back of a metal spoon.

Remove from the heat. Add peanut butter cups and softened gelatin; stir until melted. Cool quickly by placing pan in a bowl of ice water; stir for 2 minutes. Stir in evaporated milk and vanilla. Press waxed paper onto surface of custard. Refrigerate for several hours or overnight.

Fill cylinder of ice cream freezer two-thirds full; freeze according to the manufacturer's directions. Refrigerate remaining mixture until ready to freeze. When ice cream is frozen, transfer to a freezer container; freeze for 2-4 hours before serving.

YIELD: about 1 quart (8 servings)

SODA FOUNTAIN PIE

Marsha Hanson ● PONSFORD, MINNESOTA

"The first time I made this pie was during winter, using frozen berries. It was a hit even then. For a change of pace, I'm planning to make it with an Oreo cookie crust the next time."

PREP: 15 minutes + freezing

1-1/2	cups crushed sugar cones (about 12)
1/2	cup butter, melted
1/4	cup sugar
3-1/2	cups fresh strawberries, *divided*
1	quart vanilla ice cream, softened
1/3	cup malted milk powder
1-1/2	cups fudge ice cream topping, softened

Additional strawberries, optional

Combine crushed sugar cones, butter and sugar. Press onto the bottom and up the sides of an ungreased 10-in. pie plate. Freeze.

Place 3 cups of strawberries in a blender or food processor; cover and puree. Chop the remaining strawberries. Place pureed and chopped strawberries in a large bowl. Add ice cream and malted milk powder; stir to blend. Pour into prepared crust. Cover and freeze overnight.

Spread fudge topping over the pie to within 1 in. of edge; freeze for at least 2 hours. Remove from the freezer 20 minutes before serving. Serve with additional berries if desired.

YIELD: 8-10 servings

CHOCOLATE PEANUT ICE CREAM DESSERT

Jeanette Neufeld • BOISSEVAIN, MANITOBA

"If you're expecting company or simply want a convenient on-hand dessert, try this. It's easy, but people will think that you spent hours making it."

PREP: 15 minutes + freezing

- 1 cup crushed vanilla wafers
- 1/2 cup finely chopped peanuts
- 1/4 cup butter, softened
- 2 tablespoons confectioners' sugar
- 6 cups chocolate ice cream, softened, *divided*

FILLING:
- 1 package (3 ounces) cream cheese, softened
- 1/3 cup chunky peanut butter
- 3/4 cup confectioners' sugar
- 1/4 cup milk
- 1/2 cup heavy whipping cream, whipped

Line the bottom and sides of a 9-in. x 5-in. x 3-in. loaf pan with heavy-duty aluminum foil. Combine the first four ingredients; press half onto the bottom of the pan. Freeze for 15 minutes. Spread half of the ice cream over crust; freeze for 1 hour or until firm.

Meanwhile, for filling, in a large mixing bowl, beat cream cheese and peanut butter until creamy. Beat in sugar and milk. Fold in whipped cream. Spread over ice cream; freeze for 1 hour or until firm. Spread with remaining ice cream (pan will be very full). Press remaining crumb mixture on top. Cover and freeze for several hours or overnight.

Remove from the freezer 10 minutes before serving. Using foil, remove loaf from pan; discard foil. Cut into slices using a serrated knife.

YIELD: 10-12 servings

SUNSHINE SHERBET

Barbara Looney • FORT KNOX, KENTUCKY

"Together, my mother and I 'invented' this recipe. Warm, humid evenings in Georgia, where I grew up, were all the inspiration we needed! It became a favorite part of gatherings with family and friends."

PREP: 30 minutes + freezing

- 2 cups milk
- 1-1/2 cups water
- 2 cups sugar
- 2 cups heavy whipping cream
- 1-1/2 cups orange juice
- 1 can (12 ounces) evaporated milk
- 1/3 cup lemon juice
- 2 teaspoons grated orange peel
- 8 drops red food coloring, optional
- 1/2 teaspoon yellow food coloring, optional

In a large saucepan, combine the milk, water and sugar. Bring to a boil over medium heat; reduce heat. Cook and stir over for 4-5 minutes or until thickened. Remove from the heat; cool slightly. Stir in the cream, orange juice, evaporated milk, lemon juice, orange peel and food coloring if desired. Refrigerate until chilled.

Fill cylinder of ice cream freezer two-thirds full; freeze according to the manufacturer's directions. Refrigerate remaining mixture until ready to freeze. Transfer to a freezer container; freeze until firm.

YIELD: about 2 quarts (16 servings)

FUDGY NUT COFFEE PIE

Amy Theis ● BILLINGS, MONTANA

"My mother served this pretty pie for my birthday one year, and now it's one of my favorites. Fudge sauce, chopped pecans and coffee ice cream top the chocolate crumb crust. Sometimes I garnish the pie with dollops of whipped cream."

PREP: 15 minutes + freezing

1-1/2	cups confectioners' sugar
1/2	cup heavy whipping cream
6	tablespoons butter, cubed
3	squares (1 ounce *each*) unsweetened chocolate
3	tablespoons light corn syrup

Dash salt

1	teaspoon vanilla extract
1	chocolate crumb crust (9 inches)
3/4	cup coarsely chopped pecans, *divided*
3	pints coffee ice cream, softened

In a small saucepan, combine the confectioners' sugar, cream, butter, chocolate, corn syrup and salt. Cook and stir over low heat until smooth. Remove from the heat. Stir in vanilla. Cool completely.

Spread 1/2 cup fudge sauce over the crust. Sprinkle with 1/4 cup pecans. Freeze for 20 minutes or until set. Spread with half of the ice cream. Freeze for 1 hour or until firm. Repeat layers. Cover and freeze for 4 hours or until firm. Just before serving, drizzle remaining fudge sauce over pie and sprinkle with remaining pecans.

YIELD: 8 servings

HOMEMADE FROZEN CUSTARD

Judy Clark ● ELKHART, INDIANA

"My siblings and I had a hard time finding room for dessert after Mom's meals, but when we were ready, we could count on some creamy frozen custard."

PREP: 20 minutes + freezing

4	cups milk
1-1/4	cups sugar
1/3	cup cornstarch
1/8	teaspoon salt
4	eggs
1	can (14 ounces) sweetened condensed milk
2	tablespoons vanilla extract

In a large saucepan, heat milk to 175°; stir in sugar, cornstarch and salt until dissolved. Whisk a small amount of the hot mixture into the eggs. Return all to the pan, whisking constantly. Cook and stir over low heat until mixture reaches at least 160° and coats the back of a metal spoon.

Remove from the heat. Cool quickly by placing pan in a bowl of ice water; stir for 2 minutes. Stir in condensed milk and vanilla. Press waxed paper onto surface of custard. Refrigerate for several hours or overnight.

Fill cylinder of ice cream freezer two thirds full; freeze according to the manufacturer's directions. Refrigerate remaining mixture until ready to freeze. When ice cream is frozen, transfer to a freezer container; freeze for 2-4 hours before serving.

YIELD: 1-1/2 quarts (12 servings)

PINEAPPLE ICE CREAM
Phyllis Eismann Schmalz
KANSAS CITY, KANSAS

"I rely on my ice cream maker when whipping up this five-ingredient frozen treat. The creamy concoction has just the right amount of pineapple to keep guests asking for more."

PREP: 40 minutes + freezing

- 2 cups milk
- 1 cup sugar
- 3 eggs, beaten
- 1-3/4 cups heavy whipping cream
- 1 can (8 ounces) crushed pineapple, undrained

In a large saucepan, heat milk to 175°; stir in sugar until dissolved. Whisk a small amount of the hot mixture into the eggs. Return all to the pan, whisking constantly. Cook and stir over low heat until mixture reaches at least 160° and coats the back of a metal spoon.

Remove from the heat. Cool quickly by placing pan in a bowl of ice water; stir for 2 minutes. Stir in whipping cream and pineapple. Press waxed paper onto surface of custard. Refrigerate for several hours or overnight.

Fill cylinder of ice cream freezer two-thirds full; freeze according to the manufacturer's directions. Refrigerate remaining mixture until ready to freeze. When ice cream is frozen, transfer to a freezer container; freeze for 2-4 hours before serving.

YIELD: 6 servings

COFFEE ICE CREAM

Theresa Hansen • PENSACOLA, FLORIDA

"I combined two recipes—one for vanilla ice cream and the other for a special coffee sauce—to create this one. I serve it plain, just scooped into a dessert dish, so the mild, creamy coffee flavor can be enjoyed to the fullest."

PREP: 30 minutes + freezing

1/4	cup sugar
1	tablespoon cornstarch
1	tablespoon instant coffee granules
2	tablespoons butter, melted
1	cup milk
1	teaspoon vanilla extract
1	can (14 ounces) sweetened condensed milk
2	cups heavy whipping cream

In a large saucepan, combine the sugar, cornstarch, coffee and butter until blended. Stir in milk. Bring to a boil over medium heat; cook and stir for 2 minutes or until thickened. Remove from the heat; stir in vanilla. Cool completely. Stir in condensed milk.

In a large mixing bowl, beat cream until stiff peaks form; fold into milk mixture. Pour into a 9-in. pan. Cover and freeze for 6 hours or until firm.

YIELD: 1-1/2 quarts (12 servings)

FROSTY LEMON PIE

Judith Wilke • DOUSMAN, WISCONSIN

"This pie is a nice light and refreshing finish to a summer picnic or patio supper. I like that it can be made ahead and kept in the freezer."

PREP: 30 minutes + freezing

3/4	cup sugar
1/3	cup lemon juice
1/4	cup butter, cubed
Dash salt	
3	eggs, beaten
2	pints vanilla ice cream, softened, *divided*
1	graham cracker crust (9 inches)
Whipped topping, fresh mint and lemon peel, optional	

In a small saucepan, combine the sugar, lemon juice, butter and salt; cook and stir over medium heat until sugar is dissolved and the butter is melted. Whisk a small amount of sugar mixture into eggs; return all to the pan. Cook and stir over medium heat until mixture reaches 160° or is thick enough to coat the back of a metal spoon. Refrigerate until completely cooled.

Spread half of ice cream into the crust; freeze for 1 hour or until firm. Cover with half of the lemon mixture; freeze for 1 hour or until firm. Repeat layers. Cover and freeze for several hours or overnight.

Remove from the freezer 10 minutes before serving. Garnish with whipped topping, mint and lemon peel if desired.

YIELD: 8 servings

Sandwich Your Ice Cream

Place 1/2 cup of ice cream on a 3-in. cookie. Place another cookie on top. Next roll the edges in miniature chocolate chips, chopped nuts or jimmies. Wrap in plastic wrap and freeze until serving.

CANDY BAR FREEZER DESSERT

Melissa Heberer • HOSKINS, NEBRASKA

"I combine butter pecan ice cream and instant pudding to create this sweet frozen treat. A crushed Butterfinger candy bar adds crunch to the tasty topping."

PREP: 20 minutes + freezing

2 cups graham cracker crumbs
1 cup crushed saltines (about 30 crackers)
1/2 cup butter, melted
2 cups cold milk
2 packages (3.4 ounces *each*) instant vanilla pudding mix
4 cups butter pecan ice cream, softened
1 carton (8 ounces) frozen whipped topping, thawed
1 Butterfinger candy bar (2.1 ounces), chopped

In a large bowl, combine the cracker crumbs and butter. Pat three-fourths of the mixture into an ungreased 13-in. x 9-in. x 2-in. dish. Cover and refrigerate.

In a large bowl, whisk milk and pudding mixes for 2 minutes or until thickened. Stir in ice cream until blended. Spread over crust. Spread whipped topping over pudding layer.

In a small bowl, combine chopped candy bar and the remaining crumb mixture; sprinkle over whipped topping. Cover and freeze for at least 2 hours.

YIELD: 12-15 servings

ORANGE-SWIRL YOGURT PIE

Nancy Zimmerman • CAPE MAY COURT HOUSE, NEW JERSEY

"This refreshing frozen pie is an excellent grand finale to any meal. The gingersnap crust complements the frozen yogurt and citrus sauce nicely. It's great for entertaining because you make it a day early."

PREP: 25 minutes + freezing

1/4 cup sugar
4 teaspoons cornstarch
1 can (6 ounces) frozen orange juice concentrate, thawed
1/3 cup water
2 tablespoons butter
1 tablespoon grated orange peel
6 cups frozen vanilla yogurt, *divided*

CRUST:
1-1/4 cups crushed gingersnaps (about 20 cookies)
1/3 cup butter, melted

In a small saucepan, combine sugar and cornstarch. Stir in orange juice concentrate and water until smooth. Bring to a boil; cook and stir for 1-2 minutes or until thickened. Remove from the heat; stir in butter and orange peel. Cool to room temperature, stirring several times.

Soften 4 cups of frozen yogurt. Meanwhile, in a small bowl, combine gingersnaps and butter; press onto the bottom and up the sides of a greased 9-in. pie plate.

Spoon softened yogurt into crust. Top with half of the orange sauce; cut through with a knife to swirl. Place scoops of the remaining frozen yogurt over filling. Drizzle with remaining orange sauce. Cover and freeze for at least 8 hours before cutting. May be frozen for up to 3 months.

YIELD: 6-8 servings

CHAPTER 3
Refrigerated Desserts

Blueberry Angel Dessert, 60

STRAWBERRY CHIFFON PIE

Gale Spross • WILLS POINT, TEXAS

"A friend gave this recipe to me many years ago. It's guilt-free eating at its best!"

PREP: 15 minutes + chilling

1	package (.3 ounce) sugar-free strawberry gelatin
3/4	cup boiling water
1-1/4	cups cold water
1	cup frozen reduced-fat whipped topping, thawed
2-1/4	cups sliced fresh strawberries, *divided*
1	reduced-fat graham cracker crust (8 inches)

In a large bowl, dissolve gelatin in boiling water. Stir in cold water. Refrigerate until slightly thickened. Fold in the whipped topping and 2 cups of strawberries. Pour into the crust. Refrigerate for 3 hours or until set. Garnish with the remaining strawberries.

YIELD: 8 servings

BLACKBERRY NECTARINE PIE

Linda Chinn • ENUMCLAW, WASHINGTON

"Blackberries are abundant here in Washington, so I've made this pretty double-fruit pie many times. I can always tell when my husband wants me to bake this pie because he'll bring home blackberries that he picked behind his office."

PREP: 15 minutes + chilling

1/4	cup cornstarch
1	can (12 ounces) frozen unsweetened apple juice concentrate, thawed
2	cups fresh blackberries, *divided*
5	medium nectarines, peeled and coarsely chopped
1	reduced-fat graham cracker crust (8 inches)

Reduced-fat whipped topping, optional

In a small saucepan, combine cornstarch and apple juice concentrate until smooth. Bring to a boil. Add 1/2 cup of blackberries; cook and stir for 2 minutes or until thickened.

Toss the nectarines and remaining blackberries; place in the crust. Pour apple juice mixture over fruit (crust will be full). Cover and refrigerate for 8 hours or overnight. Garnish with whipped topping if desired.

YIELD: 8 servings

Facts on Fresh Berries

After buying berries, discard those that are soft, shriveled or moldy. Rinse the remaining berries and set them in a single layer in a paper towel-lined bowl. They'll keep in the fridge for 3 days.

CHOCOLATE CREAM PIE

Mary Anderson ● De Valls Bluff, Arkansas

"Our teenage son has done lots of 4-H baking. His favorite is this old-fashioned, creamy chocolate pudding in a flaky crust."

PREP: 1-1/4 hours + chilling

1-1/2	cups sugar
1/3	cup all-purpose flour
3	tablespoons baking cocoa
1/2	teaspoon salt
1-1/2	cups water
1	can (12 ounces) evaporated milk
5	egg yolks, lightly beaten
1/2	cup butter
1	teaspoon vanilla extract
1	pastry shell (9 inches), baked

Whipped topping

In a large saucepan, combine the first six ingredients. Cook and stir over medium-high heat for 2 minutes or until thickened and bubbly. Reduce heat; cook and stir 2 minutes longer. Remove from the heat. Whisk 1 cup hot mixture into egg yolks. Return all to the pan; bring to a gentle boil, stirring constantly.

Remove from the heat; stir in butter and vanilla. Cool slightly. Pour warm filling into pastry shell. Cool for 1 hour. Chill until set. Just before serving, garnish with whipped topping.

YIELD: 6-8 servings

FROSTED ORANGE PIE

Delores Edgecomb ● Atlanta, New York

"I discovered the recipe for this distinctive pie in a church cookbook. With its fresh-tasting filling and fluffy frosting, it's truly an elegant final course."

PREP: 40 minutes + chilling

3/4	cup sugar
1/2	cup all-purpose flour
1/4	teaspoon salt
1-1/4	cups water
2	egg yolks, lightly beaten
1/2	cup orange juice
2	tablespoons lemon juice
2	to 3 tablespoons grated orange peel
1/2	teaspoon grated lemon peel
1	pastry shell (9 inches), baked

FROSTING:

1/2	cup sugar
2	egg whites
2	tablespoons water
1/8	teaspoon cream of tartar
1/8	teaspoon salt
1/2	cup flaked coconut, toasted, optional

In a large saucepan, combine the sugar, flour and salt. Stir in water until smooth. Cook and stir over medium-high heat until thickened and bubbly. Reduce heat; cook and stir 2 minutes longer. Remove from the heat.

Stir a small amount of hot filling into egg yolks; return all to pan, stirring constantly. Bring to a gentle boil; cook and stir 2 minutes longer. Remove from the heat. Gently stir in the juices and orange and lemon peel. Cool to room temperature without stirring. Pour into pastry shell. Cool on a wire rack for 1 hour. Chill at least 3 hours.

In a large heavy saucepan, combine the sugar, egg whites, water, cream of tartar and salt over low heat. With a hand mixer, beat on low speed for 1 minute. Continue beating on low over low heat until frosting reaches 160°, about 8-10 minutes. Pour into a large mixing bowl. Beat on high until frosting forms stiff peaks, about 7 minutes. Spread over chilled pie. Just before serving, sprinkle with coconut if desired. Store in the refrigerator.

YIELD: 6-8 servings

Editor's Note: A stand mixer is recommended for beating the frosting after it reaches 160°.

PEACHES 'N' CREAM GELATIN DESSERT

Cyndi Brinkhause ● SOUTH COAST METRO, CALIFORNIA

"Dinner guests are never too full for this luscious dessert. You can make it ahead to cut down on last-minute fuss. Plus, the graham cracker crust, lovely peaches and pretty layers always draw raves."

PREP: 20 minutes + chilling

1-1/3   cups graham cracker crumbs (about 22 squares)
1/4   cup sugar
1/3   cup butter, melted
TOPPING:
1   package (8 ounces) cream cheese, softened
1/4   cup sugar
1/4   cup milk
1   carton (8 ounces) frozen whipped topping, thawed
1   can (15-1/4 ounces) sliced peaches, drained
1   package (3 ounces) peach gelatin
3/4   cup boiling water
1-1/4   cups cold water

In a small bowl, combine the crumbs, sugar and butter. Press into a 13-in. x 9-in. x 2-in. dish. In a large mixing bowl, beat cream cheese and sugar until smooth; gradually add the milk. Fold in the whipped topping. Spread over crust.

Cut peach slices in half lengthwise; arrange over top. In a small bowl, dissolve the gelatin in boiling water; stir in the cold water. Refrigerate for 1-1/2 hours or until slightly thickened. Gently spoon gelatin over peaches; chill until set. Cut into squares.

YIELD: 12-15 servings

CARAMEL-PECAN CHEESE PIE

Patsy Mullins ● TAFT, TENNESSEE

"Summers are hot here, so when the weather is warm, I try to use my oven as little as possible. Family and friends love this tasty no-bake pie, and no one can believe how easy it is to assemble."

PREP: 20 minutes + chilling

1   envelope unflavored gelatin
1/3   cup cold water
1/4   cup lemon juice
3   ounces reduced-fat cream cheese, cubed
1   cup nonfat dry milk powder
Sugar substitute equivalent to 2 tablespoons sugar
1   carton (8 ounces) frozen reduced-fat whipped topping, thawed
5   tablespoons chopped pecans, toasted, *divided*
1   reduced-fat graham cracker crust (9 inches)
2   tablespoons fat-free caramel ice cream topping

In a small saucepan, sprinkle gelatin over cold water; let stand for 1 minute. Heat over low heat, stirring until gelatin is dissolved. Cool slightly.

In a blender, combine the lemon juice, cream cheese and gelatin mixture; cover and process until smooth. Add milk powder and sugar substitute; cover and process for 1 minute or until blended.

Transfer to a large bowl; fold in the whipped topping. Stir in 3 tablespoons of pecans. Pour into crust. Sprinkle with remaining pecans. Drizzle with caramel topping. Cover and refrigerate for 2-3 hours or until set.

YIELD: 8 servings

Editor's Note: This recipe was tested with Splenda No Calorie Sweetener.

BLACK FOREST DESSERT

Connie Sibbing • QUINCY, ILLINOIS

"This elegant treat is a cinch to make with dessert mixes, pie filling and whipped topping. I sometimes assemble it a day beforehand and keep it in the freezer."

PREP: 25 minutes + chilling

- 1 package (11.4 ounces) no-bake chocolate lover's flavored dessert mix
- 1 package (11.1 ounces) no-bake cheesecake dessert mix
- 2 tablespoons sugar
- 2/3 cup butter, melted
- 1 carton (16 ounces) frozen whipped topping, thawed
- 1 can (21 ounces) cherry pie filling

Set aside chocolate topping pouch from the chocolate dessert mix for garnish. In a large bowl, combine contents of the crust mix packets from both mixes; add sugar and butter. Press into a 13-in. x 9-in. x 2-in. dish.

Prepare cheesecake dessert mix filling according to package directions; gently spread over crust. Prepare chocolate dessert mix filling according to package directions; carefully spread over cheesecake layer.

Spread with whipped topping. Carefully spread cherry pie filling to edges. Cover and refrigerate for at least 2 hours. Just before serving, drizzle with reserved chocolate topping. Refrigerate leftovers.

YIELD: 15 servings

Editor's Note: This recipe was tested with Jell-O no-bake dessert mixes.

CREAMY PEANUT BUTTER PIE

Rhonda McDaniel • ROSSVILLE, GEORGIA

"Quartered peanut butter cups top this rich, smooth pie that's always a hit at gatherings. It saves time because it can be made in advance and refrigerated."

PREP: 15 minutes + chilling

- 1 package (8 ounces) cream cheese, softened
- 1/2 cup sugar
- 1/3 cup creamy peanut butter
- 1/3 cup whipped topping
- 10 peanut butter cups, *divided*
- 1 chocolate crumb crust (8 *or* 9 inches)

In a small mixing bowl, beat the cream cheese, sugar and peanut butter until smooth and light. Fold in the whipped topping. Coarsely chop half of the peanut butter cups; stir into cream cheese mixture.

Spoon into crust. Quarter remaining peanut butter cups; arrange over top. Refrigerate for 4 hours before cutting.

YIELD: 6-8 servings

BLUEBERRY ANGEL DESSERT

Carol Johnson • TYLER, TEXAS

"This light, impressive dessert doesn't keep you in the kitchen for hours."

PREP: 10 minutes + chilling

- 1 package (8 ounces) cream cheese, softened
- 1 cup confectioners' sugar
- 1 carton (8 ounces) frozen whipped topping, thawed
- 1 prepared angel food cake (16 ounces), cut into 1-inch pieces
- 2 cans (21 ounces *each*) blueberry pie filling

In a large mixing bowl, beat cream cheese and sugar until smooth; fold in whipped topping and cake cubes. Spread evenly into an ungreased 13-in. x 9-in. x 2-in. dish; top with pie filling. Cover and refrigerate for at least 2 hours before cutting into squares.

YIELD: 12-15 servings

RASPBERRY DESSERT WITH VANILLA SAUCE

Marie Baumgartner
STOUGHTON, WISCONSIN

"This fruity dessert comes from my German background. We had a raspberry patch, so Mom served it when berries were in season."

PREP: 30 minutes + chilling

- 4 cups fresh *or* frozen unsweetened raspberries, thawed, crushed
- 1/2 cup orange juice
- 1/4 cup quick-cooking tapioca
- 1/2 cup sugar
- 1/8 teaspoon salt
- 2 teaspoons cornstarch
- 1 tablespoon sugar
- 1 cup 2% milk
- 1 egg, lightly beaten
- 1 teaspoon vanilla extract

In a large saucepan, combine the raspberries, orange juice and tapioca; let stand for 15 minutes. Stir in sugar and salt. Bring to a boil; cook and stir for 2 minutes or until thickened. Remove from the heat. Cover and refrigerate.

For vanilla sauce, combine cornstarch and sugar in a small saucepan; gradually stir in milk. Bring to a boil; cook and stir for 1-2 minutes or until thickened. Remove from the heat.

Whisk 1/2 cup of hot mixture into the egg; return all to the pan, whisking constantly. Cook and stir over medium-low heat for 2-3 minutes or just until the sauce thickens slightly and reaches 160° (do not boil).

Remove from the heat. Stir in vanilla. Pour into a large bowl; press a piece of waxed paper or plastic wrap over top of sauce. Refrigerate until serving. Divide raspberry mixture between four dishes; top with vanilla sauce.

YIELD: 4 servings

FLUFFY PINEAPPLE PIE

Ozela Haynes ● EMERSON, ARKANSAS

"Pineapple bits add tropical flair to this fluffy dessert. It is very light, and it isn't overly sweet. Plus, it's easy to make."

PREP: 10 minutes + chilling

>   2   cans (8 ounces *each*) crushed
>   pineapple
>   24   large marshmallows
>   2   cups whipped topping
>   1   graham cracker crust (9 inches)
> Maraschino cherries, optional

Drain pineapple, reserving 1/2 cup juice (discard remaining juice or save for another use). Set pineapple aside.

In a microwave-safe bowl, combine juice and marshmallows. Microwave, uncovered, on high 1 minute; stir. Microwave 1 minute longer or until mixture is smooth. Refrigerate 30 minutes until slightly thickened and cooled, stirring occasionally.

Fold in whipped topping and pineapple. Pour into the crust. Cover and refrigerate for 2 hours or until firm. Garnish with cherries if desired.

YIELD: 6-8 servings

COFFEE MALLOW PIE

Dorothy Smith ● EL DORADO, ARKANSAS

"This simply sophisticated pie holds up well in the refrigerator overnight."

PREP: 25 minutes + chilling

>   1   cup water
>   1   tablespoon instant coffee
>   granules
>   4   cups miniature marshmallows
>   1   tablespoon butter
>   1   cup heavy whipping cream,
>   whipped
>   1   pastry shell (9 inches), baked
>   1/2   cup chopped walnuts *or* pecans,
>   toasted
> Additional whipped cream and
>   chocolate curls, optional

In a heavy saucepan, bring water to a boil; stir in coffee until dissolved. Reduce heat; add marshmallows and butter. Cook and stir over low heat until marshmallows are melted and mixture is smooth.

Set saucepan in ice and whisk mixture constantly until cooled. Fold in whipped cream; spoon into pastry shell. Sprinkle with nuts. Refrigerate for at least 3 hours before serving. Garnish with whipped cream and chocolate curls if desired.

YIELD: 6-8 servings

Marshmallow Magic

Marshmallows are a great addition to creamy desserts. When they stick together, pour a tablespoon of confectioners' sugar in the bag. Shake the bag, and most will separate on their own.

COCONUT ANGEL SQUARES

Betty Claycomb ● ALVERTON, PENNSYLVANIA

"I have so many speedy dessert recipes, but this one is truly special. It tastes like a coconut cream pie with only a fraction of the work."

PREP: 15 minutes + chilling

1	prepared angel food cake (8 inches), cut into 1/2-inch cubes
1-1/2	cups cold milk
2	packages (3.4 ounces *each*) instant coconut cream pudding mix
1	quart vanilla ice cream, softened
1	carton (8 ounces) frozen whipped topping, thawed
1/4	cup flaked coconut, toasted

Place cake cubes in a greased 13-in. x 9-in. x 2-in. dish. In a mixing bowl, beat milk and pudding mixes on low speed for 2 minutes. Add ice cream; beat on low just until combined.

Spoon over cake cubes. Spread with whipped topping; sprinkle with coconut. Cover and chill for at least 1 hour.

YIELD: 12-15 servings

CREAMY STRAWBERRY DESSERT

Rhonda Butterbaugh ● WEATHERFORD, OKLAHOMA

"This fruity gelatin dessert is a summertime staple in my home. I usually prepare it the day before I need it. It disappears really fast!"

PREP: 25 minutes + chilling

1-1/2	cups crushed vanilla wafers
1/2	cup sugar
1/2	cup packed brown sugar
1/2	cup butter, melted
2	packages (3 ounces *each*) strawberry gelatin
1	cup boiling water
1	package (16 ounces) frozen sweetened sliced strawberries, thawed
1	can (14 ounces) sweetened condensed milk
1	carton (12 ounces) frozen whipped topping, thawed

In a bowl, combine wafer crumbs, sugars and butter; press into an ungreased 13-in. x 9-in. x 2-in. dish. Cover and refrigerate for 30 minutes.

Sprinkle gelatin over boiling water. Remove from the heat; stir until gelatin is completely dissolved, about 5 minutes. Transfer to a large bowl; stir in strawberries and milk. Refrigerate for 30 minutes or until partially set.

Fold whipped topping into strawberry mixture. Spread over prepared crust. Refrigerate for 2 hours or until set. Cut into squares.

YIELD: 15 servings

CREAMY WATERMELON PIE

Velma Beck ● CARLINVILLE, ILLINOIS

"This pie is so refreshing that it never lasts long. Watermelon and a few convenience items make it a delightful surprise that doesn't take much effort."

PREP: 15 minutes + chilling

1	package (3 ounces) watermelon gelatin
1/4	cup boiling water
1	carton (12 ounces) frozen whipped topping, thawed
2	cups cubed seeded watermelon
1	graham cracker crust (9 inches)

In a large bowl, dissolve gelatin in boiling water. Cool to room temperature. Whisk in whipped topping; fold in watermelon. Spoon into crust. Refrigerate for 2 hours or until set.

YIELD: 6-8 servings

COOL MANDARIN DESSERT

Sue Murphy
GREENWOOD, MICHIGAN

"I've served this refreshing, pleasantly light citrus dessert for years. It is easy to make but looks so elegant. For special occasions, I put it in a crystal bowl to show off its pretty color."

PREP: 20 minutes + chilling

1   can (11 ounces) mandarin oranges
2   packages (.3 ounce *each*) sugar-free orange gelatin
2   cups boiling water
1   pint orange sherbet, softened
Fresh mint, optional

Drain oranges, reserving the juice; add enough water to juice to measure 1 cup. Refrigerate the oranges.

In a large bowl, dissolve gelatin in boiling water. Stir in reserved juice. Add sherbet, stirring until dissolved. Refrigerate for 1 hour or until thickened.

Keep 10 orange segments refrigerated for garnish. Fold remaining oranges into gelatin mixture; cover and refrigerate overnight. Just before serving, garnish with reserved oranges and mint if desired.

YIELD: 10 servings

LIGHT LEMON PIE

Ruby Fleeman • Santa Ana, Texas

"A drizzle of spreadable fruit lends a decorative and tasty touch to this appealing dessert. One slice of the creamy pie just won't be enough! My entire family really enjoys it."

PREP: 20 minutes + chilling

1 package (.3 ounces) sugar-free lemon gelatin
1/2 cup boiling water
3/4 cup cold water
Sugar substitute equivalent to 3 tablespoons plus 1 teaspoon sugar
1 cup (8 ounces) 1% cottage cheese
1 carton (8 ounces) frozen reduced-fat whipped topping, thawed
1 reduced-fat graham cracker crust (8 inches)
1/2 cup 100% strawberry spreadable fruit
8 large strawberries, halved

In a large bowl, dissolve gelatin in boiling water. Stir in cold water and sugar substitute. Refrigerate until partially set.

In a fine strainer, drain the cottage cheese. Place cottage cheese in a blender; cover and process until smooth. Transfer to a bowl; stir in gelatin mixture. Fold in whipped topping.

Pour into crust. Refrigerate until set. Just before serving, cut into slices; garnish each with 1 tablespoon spreadable fruit and two strawberry halves.

YIELD: 8 servings

Editor's Note: This recipe was tested with Splenda No Calorie Sweetener.

CREAMY GELATIN DESSERT

Janis Garrett • Macon, Georgia

"This yummy recipe from my husband's sister is a favorite whenever we get together with our five married children."

PREP: 20 minutes + chilling

1 package (6 ounces) lemon gelatin
2 cups boiling water
2 cups miniature marshmallows
4 large ripe bananas, cut into 1/4-inch slices
1 can (20 ounces) crushed pineapple
2 cups cold water
1/2 cup sugar
2 tablespoons all-purpose flour
2 tablespoons butter
1 cup heavy whipping cream
1/2 cup chopped walnuts

Sprinkle gelatin over boiling water. Remove from the heat; stir until gelatin is completely dissolved, about 5 minutes. Stir in marshmallows until melted. Stir in bananas. Drain pineapple, reserving juice. Add pineapple and cold water to the gelatin mixture.

Pour into a 13-in. x 9-in. x 2-in. pan; chill until set. In a small saucepan, combine the sugar and flour. Gradually stir in reserved pineapple juice. Add butter; bring to a boil. Cook and stir for 2 minutes. Remove from the heat; cool to room temperature, about 35-40 minutes.

In a small mixing bowl, beat the cream until firm peaks form; fold into pineapple juice mixture. Spread over gelatin mixture. Sprinkle with nuts. Chill for 1-2 hours.

YIELD: 16-20 servings

RASPBERRY ICEBOX DESSERT

Magdalene Dyck • BURNS LAKE, BRITISH COLUMBIA

"After tasting this dessert at a church social, I just had to track down the recipe. I was thrilled to learn how easy it is to make. With its smooth pudding layer and colorful berry topping, it's a hit with everyone who tries it."

PREP: 20 minutes + chilling

2	packages (3 ounces *each*) raspberry gelatin
2	cups boiling water
3	cups fresh *or* frozen raspberries
2	cups graham cracker crumbs (about 32 squares)
1/4	cup packed brown sugar
1/2	cup butter, melted
1-1/2	cups cold milk
1	package (3.4 ounces) instant vanilla pudding mix
1	package (8 ounces) cream cheese, softened

In a large bowl, combine the gelatin and water; stir until gelatin is dissolved. Fold in the raspberries. Refrigerate for 1 hour or until syrupy.

In a small bowl, combine the cracker crumbs, brown sugar and butter. Press into a greased 13-in. x 9-in. x 2-in. dish. In a large mixing bowl, beat the milk and pudding mix on low speed for 2 minutes.

In another mixing bowl, beat cream cheese until smooth. Gradually add pudding. Spread over crust. Spoon gelatin mixture over top. Chill until set.

YIELD: 12-15 servings

TIN ROOF FUDGE PIE

Cynthia Kolberg • SYRACUSE, INDIANA

"This delectable pie makes a great hostess gift for a holiday get-together or a wonderful ending to a meal for company."

PREP: 30 minutes + chilling

2	squares (1 ounce *each*) semisweet baking chocolate
1	tablespoon butter
1	pastry shell (9 inches), baked

PEANUT LAYER:

20	caramels
1/3	cup heavy whipping cream
1-1/2	cups salted peanuts

CHOCOLATE LAYER:

8	squares (1 ounce *each*) semisweet chocolate, coarsely chopped
2	tablespoons butter
1	cup heavy whipping cream
2	teaspoons vanilla extract
	Whipped cream and salted peanuts, optional

TOPPING:

3	caramels
5	teaspoons heavy whipping cream
1	tablespoon butter

In a small saucepan, melt chocolate and butter over low heat, stirring until smooth. Spread onto the bottom and up the sides of crust; refrigerate the crust until the chocolate is set.

For peanut layer, in a small saucepan, melt caramels and cream over low heat, stirring frequently until smooth. Remove from the heat; stir in peanuts. Spoon into the pie shell; refrigerate.

For chocolate layer, in a small saucepan, melt chocolate and butter over low heat, stirring until smooth. Remove from the heat; let stand for 15 minutes.

Meanwhile, in a large mixing bowl, beat cream and vanilla until soft peaks form. Carefully fold a third of the whipped cream into the chocolate mixture; fold in the remaining whipped cream. Spread over peanut layer; refrigerate until set. Garnish with whipped cream and peanuts if desired.

For topping, in a small saucepan, melt caramels, cream and butter over low heat, stirring until smooth. Drizzle over pie. Store in the refrigerator.

YIELD: 8-10 servings

MINI CARAMEL CHEESECAKES

Taste of Home Test Kitchen

"Using individual graham cracker shells makes it easy to prepare these treats. They taste just like cheesecake without all the hassle."

PREP: 20 minutes + chilling

- 1 package (8 ounces) cream cheese, softened
- 2 tablespoons apple juice concentrate
- 2 tablespoons sugar
- 1/4 cup caramel ice cream topping
- 1/2 cup whipped topping
- 1 package (6 count) individual graham cracker tart shells

Additional caramel ice cream topping, optional

Chopped almonds *or* honey roasted almonds, optional

In a large mixing bowl, beat the cream cheese, apple juice concentrate, sugar and ice cream topping until smooth. Fold in whipped topping.

Spoon into tart shells. Drizzle with additional ice cream topping and sprinkle with almonds if desired. Refrigerate until serving.

YIELD: 6 servings ·

EASY TIRAMISU

Nancy Brown ● DAHINDA, ILLINOIS

"This no-bake treat comes together quickly and can even be made the night before you plan on serving it."

PREP: 20 minutes + chilling

- 1 package (10-3/4 ounces) frozen pound cake, thawed
- 3/4 cup strong brewed coffee
- 1 package (8 ounces) cream cheese, softened
- 1 cup sugar
- 1/2 cup chocolate syrup
- 1 cup heavy whipping cream, whipped
- 2 Heath candy bars (1.4 ounces *each*), crushed

Cut cake into nine slices. Arrange in an ungreased 11-in. x 7-in. x 2-in. dish, cutting to fit if needed. Drizzle with coffee. In a mixing bowl, beat cream cheese and sugar until smooth. Add chocolate syrup. Fold in whipped cream. Spread over cake. Sprinkle with candy bars. Refrigerate until serving.

YIELD: 8 servings

MAKE-AHEAD SHORTCAKE

Karen Ann Bland ● GOVE, KANSAS

"This classic has all the satisfaction of traditional strawberry shortcake."

PREP: 15 minutes + chilling

- 1 loaf (14 ounces) angel food cake, cut into 1-inch slices
- 1/2 cup cold milk
- 1 package (5.1 ounces) instant vanilla pudding mix
- 1 pint vanilla ice cream, softened
- 1 package (6 ounces) strawberry gelatin
- 1 cup boiling water
- 2 packages (10 ounces *each*) frozen sweetened sliced strawberries

Sliced fresh strawberries, optional

Arrange cake slices in a single layer in an ungreased 13-in. x 9-in. x 2-in. dish. In a large mixing bowl, beat milk and pudding mix for 2 minutes or until thickened; beat in ice cream. Pour over cake. Chill.

In a bowl, dissolve gelatin in boiling water; stir in frozen strawberries. Chill until partially set. Spoon over pudding mixture. Chill until firm. Garnish with fresh berries if desired.

YIELD: 12 servings

PEACH ANGEL DESSERT

Marge Hubrich • St. Cloud, Minnesota

"This light and lovely dessert is absolutely heavenly! Try it with fresh strawberries, raspberries or blueberries, using the corresponding flavor of gelatin. It's delicious with any pairing you choose."

PREP: 20 minutes + chilling

- 3/4 **cup sugar**
- 2 **tablespoons cornstarch**
- 1 **cup water**
- 2 **tablespoons corn syrup**
- 1/4 **cup peach, apricot *or* orange gelatin powder**
- 1 **loaf (10-1/2 ounces) angel food cake**
- 1 **package (8 ounces) reduced-fat cream cheese**
- 2/3 **cup confectioners' sugar**
- 2 **tablespoons fat-free milk**
- 1 **carton (8 ounces) frozen reduced-fat whipped topping, thawed**
- 3 **cups sliced peeled fresh *or* frozen peaches, thawed**

In a small saucepan, combine sugar and cornstarch. Gradually whisk in water and corn syrup until smooth. Bring to a boil. Cook and stir for 1-2 minutes or until thickened. Remove from the heat; stir in gelatin until dissolved. Cool to room temperature, stirring several times.

Cut angel food cake into nine slices. Line an ungreased 13-in. x 9-in. x 2-in. dish with the slices; set aside. In a large mixing bowl, beat cream cheese and confectioners' sugar until smooth. Gradually beat in milk.

Set aside 1/3 cup whipped topping for garnish. Fold remaining whipped topping into cream cheese mixture; spread over cake. Top with peaches. Pour gelatin mixture over peaches.

Cover and refrigerate for at least 4 hours. Cut into squares. Top each piece with about 1 teaspoon of reserved whipped topping.

YIELD: 15 servings

NO-BAKE CHOCOLATE CHEESECAKE

Pat Pierce • Epworth, Iowa

"Milky Way candy bars and make-ahead convenience give this sweet specialty its fantastic flair. Our children and their families love the eye-appealing dessert."

PREP: 50 minutes + chilling

- 1 **cup cold milk**
- 1 **envelope unflavored gelatin**
- 4 **Milky Way candy bars (2.05 ounces *each*), sliced**
- 1-1/2 **cups finely crushed chocolate wafers**
- 1/4 **cup butter, melted**
- 2 **packages (8 ounces *each*) cream cheese, softened**
- 2 **tablespoons sugar**
- 1 **teaspoon vanilla extract**
- 1 **cup heavy whipping cream**

Whipped topping and fresh raspberries *or* fresh strawberries

In a medium saucepan, combine the milk and gelatin; let stand for 1 minute. Add the candy bars; cook and stir over medium heat for 5 minutes or until the candy is melted and the gelatin is dissolved. Cool to room temperature, about 45 minutes.

Meanwhile, in a small bowl, combine wafer crumbs and butter. Press onto the bottom and 1 in. up the sides of a greased 9-in. springform pan; set aside.

In a large mixing bowl, beat the cream cheese, sugar and vanilla until smooth. Add the chocolate mixture and cream. Beat on high speed for 4 minutes. Pour mixture into prepared crust. Cover and refrigerate for 8 hours or overnight.

Carefully run a knife around edge of pan to loosen. Remove sides of pan. Garnish with the whipped topping and the berries.

YIELD: 8-10 servings

STRAWBERRY BANANA DESSERT

Margaret Kuntz
BISMARCK, NORTH DAKOTA

"This treat has a bright cheery color and plenty of fruity flavor."

PREP: 15 minutes + chilling

- 3 medium firm bananas, sliced
- 1 prepared angel food cake (16 ounces), cut into 1-inch cubes
- 1 pint fresh strawberries, halved
- 1 package (.6 ounce) sugar-free strawberry gelatin
- 2 cups boiling water
- 1-1/2 cups cold water
- 1 carton (8 ounces) reduced-fat whipped topping, thawed

Layer bananas and cake in a 13-in. x 9-in. x 2-in. dish coated with cooking spray. Place berries over cake and press gently. Dissolve gelatin in boiling water; stir in cold water. Pour over berries. Refrigerate 3 hours or until set. Frost with whipped topping.

YIELD: 16 servings

CHERRY BANANA CREAM PIE

Denise Elder • HANOVER, ONTARIO

"This dessert has a crunchy crust that is spread with a rich butter layer and topped with a filling flavored with banana, cherries and chocolate. Guests tell me the pie reminds them of a banana split...and then ask for seconds."

PREP: 20 minutes + chilling

3/4	cup butter, *divided*
2	cups crushed vanilla wafers (about 60)
3/4	cup confectioners' sugar

FILLING:

1	cup heavy whipping cream
1/4	cup sugar
2	tablespoons baking cocoa
1	cup chopped walnuts
1	large firm banana, thinly sliced
1/3	cup halved maraschino cherries

Whipped topping, chocolate curls and additional maraschino cherries

In a small saucepan, melt 1/2 cup of butter; stir in wafer crumbs. Press into a 9-in. pie plate. In a small mixing bowl, cream the remaining butter and confectioners' sugar until light and fluffy. Spread over crust.

In a large mixing bowl, beat cream until it begins to thicken. Add the sugar and cocoa; beat until stiff peaks form. Fold in the walnuts, banana and maraschino cherries.

Spoon into crust. Cover and refrigerate for 8 hours or overnight. Garnish with whipped topping, chocolate curls and cherries.

YIELD: 6-8 servings

LEMON BLUEBERRY CHEESECAKE

Julia Klee • BONAIRE, GEORGIA

"For a light, refreshing alternative to traditional cheesecake, try this lovely no-bake treat."

PREP: 30 minutes + chilling

1	package (3 ounces) lemon gelatin
1	cup boiling water
1	cup graham cracker crumbs
2	tablespoons butter, melted
1	tablespoon vegetable oil
3	cups (24 ounces) fat-free cottage cheese
1/4	cup sugar

TOPPING:

2	tablespoons sugar
1-1/2	teaspoons cornstarch
1/4	cup water
1-1/3	cups fresh *or* frozen blueberries, *divided*
1	teaspoon lemon juice

In a large bowl, dissolve gelatin in boiling water. Cool. In a small bowl, combine the crumbs, butter and oil. Press onto the bottom of a 9-in. springform pan. Chill.

In a blender, process cottage cheese and sugar until smooth. While processing, slowly add cooled gelatin. Pour into crust; cover cheesecake and refrigerate overnight.

For topping, in a small saucepan, combine sugar and cornstarch; gradually stir in water until smooth. Add 1 cup blueberries. Bring to a boil; cook and stir for 2 minutes or until thickened. Stir in lemon juice; cool slightly. Transfer to a blender; cover and process until smooth. Refrigerate until chilled.

Carefully run a knife around edge of pan to loosen the cheesecake; remove the sides of pan. Spread the blueberry mixture over the top. Top with the remaining blueberries.

YIELD: 12 servings

BANANA CHEESECAKE DESSERT

Jessica Simerly • New Castle, Indiana

"I use convenience items to create a layered crowd-pleaser that features cheesecake, bananas, and chocolate and caramel sauces. Once you serve this, you'll be asked to prepare it time and again."

Prep: 25 minutes + chilling

2 packages (21.4 ounces *each*) strawberry no-bake cheesecake mix
3/4 cup butter, melted
1/4 cup sugar
3 cups cold milk
1 can (8 ounces) crushed pineapple, well drained
3 medium firm bananas, sliced
1/2 cup chocolate ice cream topping, warmed, *divided*
1/2 cup caramel ice cream topping, *divided*
1 carton (8 ounces) frozen whipped topping, thawed
1/3 cup chopped pecans
Maraschino cherries with stems

Set aside filling and strawberry topping packets from cheesecake mixes. Place the contents of the crust mix packets in a large bowl; stir in butter and sugar until crumbly. Press into an ungreased 13-in. x 9-in. x 2-in. dish.

In a large mixing bowl, beat milk and contents of filling packets on low speed until blended. Beat on high for 3 minutes or until slightly thickened. Spread over the crust. Cover and refrigerate for 1 hour.

Spread contents of strawberry topping packets over cheesecake. Top with pineapple and bananas. Drizzle with 1/4 cup of chocolate topping and 1/4 cup caramel topping. Spread with whipped topping (dish will be full). Refrigerate for 2 hours or until set. Before serving, drizzle with remaining chocolate and caramel toppings. Top with pecans and cherries.

Yield: 16-20 servings

SUMMER BERRY CHEESE PIE

Mrs. C. Florkewicz • Caldwell, New Jersey

"I love to make this pie with fresh blueberries and strawberries from area farms. It's an easy summer treat that my family just gobbles up."

Prep: 25 minutes + chilling

1 pint fresh strawberries, sliced, *divided*
1 tablespoon lemon juice
2/3 cup sugar, *divided*
1 package (8 ounces) cream cheese, softened
1 teaspoon grated lemon peel
1 graham cracker crust (9 inches)
2 tablespoons cornstarch
3 to 4 drops red food coloring, optional
1 pint fresh blueberries

In a large bowl, combine half of the strawberries and lemon juice; mash berries. Add 1/3 cup plus 2 tablespoons sugar; set aside. In a large mixing bowl, combine the cream cheese, lemon peel and remaining sugar until smooth. Spread into the crust.

In a large saucepan, combine cornstarch and reserved strawberry mixture until blended. Bring to a boil; cook and stir for 2 minutes or until thickened. Stir in food coloring if desired. Cool slightly. Fold in blueberries and remaining strawberries. Spread over cream cheese mixture. Cover and refrigerate for at least 3 hours.

Yield: 6-8 servings

CREAMY CANDY BAR DESSERT

Kathy Kittell
Lenexa, Kansas

"Here's a sweet you'll have a hard time resisting until the end of the meal. One taste and you'll smile like a kid in a candy store!"

Prep: 30 minutes + chilling

- 2 cups graham cracker crumbs
- 3 tablespoons sugar
- 1/2 cup butter, melted
- 1 jar (11-3/4 ounces) hot fudge ice cream topping

FILLING:

- 1/2 cup cold milk
- 2 packages (3.4 ounces *each*) instant vanilla *or* chocolate pudding mix
- 2 cartons (16 ounces *each*) frozen whipped topping, thawed
- 6 to 7 (2.07 ounces *each*) Snickers candy bars, chopped, *divided*

In a small bowl, combine the cracker crumbs and sugar; stir in butter. Press into an ungreased 13-in. x 9-in. x 2-in. dish. In a small saucepan, heat the fudge topping over low heat until warmed; pour evenly over crust. Cool.

In a large mixing bowl, beat the milk, pudding mix and whipped topping for 2-3 minutes or until stiff, scraping sides of bowl often. Stir in three-fourths of the candy bar pieces. Pour over crust. Sprinkle with remaining candy bar pieces. Cover and refrigerate for 2-3 hours or overnight.

Yield: 15 servings

BANANA BERRY TARTS

Barbara Nowakowski ● North Tonawanda, New York

"*If you need a no-fuss dessert that will please kids but is elegant enough for a grown-up gathering, try these tarts.*"

PREP: 10 minutes + chilling

4 ounces cream cheese, softened
2 tablespoons honey
1 package (10 ounces) frozen sweetened raspberries, thawed and undrained
1 cup miniature marshmallows
1 medium firm banana, chopped
1 cup whipped topping
1 package (6 count) individual graham cracker tart shells

In a small mixing bowl, beat cream cheese and honey until smooth; beat in raspberries until blended. Stir in marshmallows and banana. Fold in whipped topping. Spoon into tart shells. Chill until serving.

YIELD: 6 servings

LIME CHIFFON DESSERT

Joyce Key ● Snellville, Georgia

"*Originally, this make-ahead called for lemon gelatin, but we like it with lime.*"

PREP: 20 minutes + chilling

1-1/2 cups crushed graham crackers (about 24 squares)
1/3 cup sugar
1/2 cup butter, melted
FILLING:
1 package (3 ounces) lime gelatin
1 cup boiling water
2 packages (one 8 ounces, one 3 ounces) cream cheese, softened
1 cup sugar
1 teaspoon vanilla extract
1 carton (16 ounces) frozen whipped topping, thawed

Combine the first three ingredients; set aside 2 tablespoons for topping. Press remaining crumbs onto the bottom of an ungreased 13-in. x 9-in. x 2-in. baking dish; set aside. In a small bowl, dissolve gelatin in boiling water; cool.

In a large mixing bowl, beat cream cheese and sugar until smooth. Beat in vanilla. Slowly add gelatin until combined. Fold in whipped topping. Spoon over crust; sprinkle with reserved crumbs. Cover and refrigerate for 3 hours or until set.

YIELD: 12-15 servings

WHITE CHOCOLATE PIE

Sue Brown ● Hanover, Indiana

"*I tint whipped topping pink when I serve this pie on Valentine's Day.*"

PREP: 20 minutes + chilling

1 package (8 ounces) cream cheese, softened
3/4 cup confectioners' sugar
1 carton (8 ounces) frozen whipped toping, thawed, *divided*
1 chocolate crumb crust (8 inches)
1-1/4 cups cold milk
1 package (3.3 ounces) instant white chocolate pudding mix
Red food coloring

In a large mixing bowl, beat the cream cheese, confectioners' sugar and 1/4 cup whipped topping until smooth. Spread over crust.

In a small mixing bowl, beat milk and pudding mix on low speed for 2 minutes. Let stand for 2 minutes or until soft-set. Pour over cream cheese mixture. Refrigerate for 2 hours or until firm. Tint remaining whipped topping with red food coloring. Spread over pie before serving.

YIELD: 6-8 servings

APPLE CHEESECAKE

Adeline Piscitelli ● SAYREVILLE, NEW JERSEY

"With its applesauce and peanut topping, this no-bake treat hits the spot."

PREP: 35 minutes + chilling

2	envelopes unflavored gelatin
1/3	cup cold water
1-3/4	cups apple juice
1/2	cup sugar
3	egg yolks, lightly beaten
3	packages (8 ounces *each*) cream cheese, softened
1/2	teaspoon ground cinnamon
1/4	teaspoon ground nutmeg
1	cup heavy whipping cream, whipped

TOPPING:

1/2	cup chopped dry roasted peanuts
2	tablespoons butter
1	cup applesauce
1/3	cup packed brown sugar
1/4	teaspoon ground cinnamon

Additional whipped cream, cinnamon and peanuts, optional

In a small saucepan, sprinkle gelatin over cold water; let stand for 1 minute. Heat over low heat, stirring until gelatin is dissolved; set aside.

In a large saucepan, combine the apple juice and sugar until smooth. Bring to a boil over medium heat; cool slightly. Whisk a small amount of hot mixture into the egg yolks. Return all to the pan, whisking constantly. Cook and stir over medium-high heat until thickened and bubbly. Remove from the heat. Cool to room temperature.

In a mixing bowl, beat cream cheese, cinnamon and nutmeg until smooth. Gradually beat in gelatin mixture until smooth. Chill for 20 minutes or until slightly thickened. Fold in cream. Pour into an ungreased 9-in. springform pan. Chill 4 hours.

In a saucepan over medium heat, brown peanuts in butter for 2 minutes. Add the applesauce, brown sugar and cinnamon; cook and stir for 5 minutes or until heated through. Cool. Spread over top of cheesecake. Garnish with additional whipped cream, cinnamon and peanuts if desired.

YIELD: 12-16 servings

CHOCOLATE CREAM DESSERT

Laurie Muhle ● LAKE PARK, MINNESOTA

"Since the 1960s, whenever I've asked my family what dessert I should fix, this is what they've requested. It has a light texture and alluring chocolate color."

PREP: 20 minutes + chilling

3	cups crushed vanilla wafers
2/3	cup butter, melted
1/4	cup sugar
1/2	teaspoon ground cinnamon

FILLING:

1	milk chocolate candy bar (7 ounces), plain *or* with almonds, broken into pieces
1	package (10 ounces) large marshmallows
1	cup milk
2	cups heavy whipping cream, whipped
1/2	teaspoon vanilla extract

Sliced almonds, toasted, optional

In a large bowl, combine the vanilla crumbs, butter, sugar and cinnamon. Set aside 1/3 cup for topping. Press remaining crumb mixture into a greased 13-in. x 9-in. x 2-in. pan; refrigerate until firm.

In a large saucepan, heat the candy bar, marshmallows and milk over medium-low heat until chocolate and marshmallows are melted, stirring often. Remove from the heat; cool to room temperature.

Fold in whipped cream and vanilla; pour over crust. Chill for 3-4 hours. Sprinkle with reserved crumb mixture and almonds if desired.

YIELD: 12-16 servings

APRICOT DELIGHT

Alice Case • CARROLLTON, TEXAS

"With bits of angel food cake and a cream cheese-like texture, these squares taste so rich no one will guess they are light."

PREP: 15 minutes + chilling

- 2 cans (5-1/2 ounces *each*) apricot nectar, *divided*
- 1 package (.3 ounces) sugar-free orange gelatin
- 1 package (1 ounce) sugar-free instant vanilla pudding mix
- 2/3 cup nonfat dry milk powder
- 1 carton (8 ounces) frozen reduced-fat whipped topping, thawed
- 1 loaf (5 ounces) angel food cake, cubed
- 1 can (15 ounces) reduced-sugar apricot halves, drained and sliced

In a microwave-safe bowl, microwave 1 cup apricot nectar on high for 50-60 seconds or until hot. Sprinkle gelatin over hot nectar; stir until gelatin is completely dissolved, about 5 minutes. Set aside to cool.

In a large bowl, combine remaining apricot nectar and enough water to measure 1-1/4 cups; whisk in pudding mix and milk powder for 1-2 minutes. Let stand for 2 minutes or until soft-set. Whisk in cooled gelatin; fold in whipped topping and cake.

Pour into an 11-in. x 7-in. x 2-in. dish. Refrigerate for 2-4 hours. Garnish with apricot slices.

YIELD: 8 servings

CHOCOLATE MINT ECLAIR DESSERT

Renee Ratcliffe • CHARLOTTE, NORTH CAROLINA

"I think this incredible combination of mint and chocolate is just perfect for the holidays."

PREP: 20 minutes + chilling

- 23 whole chocolate graham crackers
- 3 cups cold fat-free milk
- 2 packages (3.3 to 3.4 ounces *each*) instant white chocolate *or* vanilla pudding mix
- 1/2 teaspoon mint *or* peppermint extract
- 3 to 4 drops green food coloring, optional
- 1 carton (8 ounces) frozen reduced-fat whipped topping, thawed

CHOCOLATE FROSTING:
- 1 tablespoon butter
- 2 tablespoons baking cocoa
- 2 tablespoons plus 1 teaspoon fat-free milk
- 1 teaspoon vanilla extract
- 1 cup confectioners' sugar

Coat a 13-in. x 9-in. x 2-in. dish with cooking spray. Break five whole graham crackers in half; line the bottom of pan with three half crackers and six whole crackers.

In a large bowl, whisk milk and pudding mix for 2 minutes. Let stand for 2 minutes or until soft-set. Whisk in extract and food coloring if desired. Fold in whipped topping.

Spread half over graham crackers. Top with another layer of three half and six whole crackers. Top with remaining pudding mixture and graham crackers (save remaining half cracker for another use). Cover and refrigerate for 2 hours.

For frosting, melt butter in a saucepan. Stir in cocoa and milk until blended. Remove from the heat; stir in vanilla and confectioners' sugar until smooth. Spread over dessert. Cover and refrigerate overnight.

YIELD: 15 servings

Puddings, Parfaits & More

Angel Berry Trifle, 87

BUTTERSCOTCH PARFAITS

Judi Klee ● NEBRASKA CITY, NEBRASKA

"These yummy parfaits are impossible to turn down. You can also change the pudding flavor to suit your taste."

PREP: 10 minutes + chilling

- 2 **cups cold milk**
- 1 **package (3.4 ounces) instant butterscotch pudding mix**
- 18 **vanilla wafers, coarsely crushed**
- 1 **carton (8 ounces) frozen whipped topping, thawed**
- 6 **maraschino cherries, optional**

In a large mixing bowl, beat milk and pudding mix for 2 minutes or until thickened. In six parfait glasses, alternate layers of pudding, wafer crumbs and whipped topping. Garnish with a cherry if desired. Refrigerate until serving.

YIELD: 6 servings

CAPPUCCINO MOUSSE TRIFLE

Tracy Bergland ● PRIOR LAKE, MINNESOTA

"This is the easiest trifle I've ever made, yet it looks like I spent hours on it. It gets rave reviews."

PREP: 35 minutes + chilling

- 2-1/2 **cups cold milk**
- 1/3 **cup instant coffee granules**
- 2 **packages (3.4 ounces *each*) instant vanilla pudding mix**
- 1 **carton (16 ounces) frozen whipped topping, thawed, *divided***
- 2 **loaves (10-3/4 ounces *each*) frozen pound cake, thawed and cubed**
- 1 **square (1 ounce) semisweet chocolate, grated**
- 1/4 **teaspoon ground cinnamon**

In a large mixing bowl, stir milk and coffee granules until dissolved; remove 1 cup and set aside. Add pudding mixes to the remaining milk mixture; beat on low speed for 2 minutes or until thickened. Fold in half of the whipped topping.

Place a third of the cake cubes in a 4-qt. serving or trifle bowl. Layer with a third of the reserved milk mixture and pudding mixture and a fourth of the grated chocolate. Repeat layers twice. Garnish with remaining whipped topping and chocolate. Sprinkle with cinnamon. Cover and refrigerate until serving.

YIELD: 16-20 servings

CHILLED STRAWBERRY CREAM

Ann Main ● MOOREFIELD, ONTARIO

"Made with only three ingredients, this cool, refreshing dessert goes together in a jiffy, but it's pretty enough to serve for a special occasion."

PREP: 10 minutes + chilling

- 2 **cups frozen unsweetened whole strawberries**
- 1/4 **cup confectioners' sugar**
- 1/2 **cup heavy whipping cream**

Place the strawberries and sugar in a food processor; cover and process until finely chopped.

In a small mixing bowl, beat cream until stiff peaks form. Fold into berries. Pour into serving dishes. Refrigerate or freeze for 25 minutes.

YIELD: 2 servings

DARK CHOCOLATE PUDDING

Lillian Julow ● GAINESVILLE, FLORIDA

"This rich, old-fashioned treat is oh-so creamy and comforting!"

PREP: 25 minutes + chilling

    1/4   cup sugar
      3   tablespoons cornstarch
    1/4   teaspoon salt
      2   cups milk
      3   egg yolks, lightly beaten
      1   dark chocolate candy bar
          (7 ounces), melted
    1/2   teaspoon vanilla extract
**Whipped cream, grated chocolate and
    Pirouette cookies**

In a large saucepan, combine the sugar, cornstarch and salt. Stir in milk until smooth. Cook and stir over medium-high heat until thickened and bubbly. Reduce heat; cook and stir 2 minutes longer. Remove from the heat.

Stir a small amount of hot mixture into egg yolks. Return all to pan and bring to a gentle boil, stirring constantly. Remove from the heat; gradually whisk in melted chocolate and vanilla until smooth.

Press plastic wrap onto surface of pudding. Refrigerate until serving. Spoon into dessert dishes. Garnish with whipped cream, grated chocolate and cookies.

YIELD: 4-6 servings

ALMOND CREME

Marcie McEachern ● DALLAS, TEXAS

*"My mother often made this velvety dessert for New Year's Eve.
Now that I'm married, I plan to carry on the tradition."*

PREP: 5 minutes COOK: 15 minutes + chilling

      2   envelopes unflavored gelatin
    1/2   cup water
      3   cups heavy whipping cream
      1   cup sugar
      4   eggs, lightly beaten
      1   teaspoon almond extract
**Fresh raspberries and chocolate curls,
    optional**

In a large saucepan, sprinkle gelatin over water. Let stand for 1 minute. Stir in cream and sugar. Cook and stir over medium-low heat for 5 minutes or until gelatin is completely dissolved.

Remove from the heat. Stir a small amount of hot mixture into eggs; return all to the pan, stirring constantly. Cook and stir over medium heat until a thermometer reads 160° and coats the back of a metal spoon (do not boil). Remove from the heat. Stir in almond extract.

Pour into dessert dishes. Refrigerate until set. Garnish with raspberries and chocolate curls if desired.

YIELD: 8 servings

PEAR PARFAITS

Heather Kobe ● VANCOUVER, WASHINGTON

*"It's a snap to make these parfaits since they're comprised of only four
ingredients. My husband and I regularly enjoy the handy dessert."*

PREP: 10 minutes + chilling

  1-1/2   cups vanilla yogurt
    1/4   cup confectioners' sugar
      2   cans (15-1/4 ounces *each*) sliced
          pears, well drained
  1-1/4   cups cinnamon graham cracker
          crumbs (about 7 whole crackers)

In a small bowl, combine yogurt and sugar. Place three to four pear slices each in four parfait glasses; top each with 2 tablespoons cracker crumbs and 3 tablespoons yogurt mixture. Repeat layers. Sprinkle with remaining crumbs. Refrigerate until serving.

YIELD: 4 servings

PEACH MOUSSE

Launa Shoemaker • MIDLAND CITY, ALABAMA

"This creamy mousse is a light and refreshing finish for a special meal. A garnish of peach slices or other fresh fruit really dresses up individual servings."

PREP: 20 minutes + chilling

- 1 package (3 ounces) peach *or* orange gelatin
- 1 cup boiling water
- 3 medium ripe peaches, sliced
- 2 tablespoons honey
- 1/4 teaspoon almond extract
- 1/2 cup heavy whipping cream, whipped *or* 1 cup whipped topping

Fresh mint and additional peach slices, optional

In a large mixing bowl, dissolve gelatin in water. In a blender, combine the peaches, honey and extract; cover and process until smooth. Stir into gelatin mixture. Cover and refrigerate until syrupy, about 1-1/2 hours.

In a large mixing bowl, beat peach mixture on high speed for about 5 minutes or until doubled in volume. Fold in whipped cream. Spoon into dessert dishes. Refrigerate until firm, about 1 hour. Garnish with mint and additional peaches if desired.

YIELD: 8 servings

PRETTY PLUM PARFAITS

Norma Reynolds • YORK, PENNSYLVANIA

"With a plum tree in our backyard, I'm always eager to try new plum recipes. None of them have beat this wonderful snack!"

PREP: 15 minutes COOK: 15 minutes + chilling

- 9 to 12 medium ripe red *or* purple plums (2 pounds), sliced
- 1/2 cup red currant jelly
- 1/2 cup packed brown sugar
- 1 orange peel strip (1 to 3 inches)
- 1 cinnamon stick (3 inches)
- 1 cup heavy whipping cream
- 1 tablespoon confectioners' sugar
- 1/2 teaspoon vanilla extract

Fancy cookies and additional whipped cream and plum slices, optional

In a large heavy saucepan, combine the plums, jelly, brown sugar, orange peel and cinnamon stick. Bring to a boil. Reduce heat; simmer, uncovered, for 10-15 minutes or until plums are tender, stirring occasionally. Remove from the heat; cool slightly. Discard orange peel and cinnamon stick; coarsely mash plums. Cover plumbs and refrigerate.

Just before serving, in a small mixing bowl, beat cream until it begins to thicken. Add sugar and vanilla; beat until peaks form. Place about 1/4 cup plum mixture each in four chilled parfait glasses; top with 1/4 cup whipped cream. Repeat layers. Top with remaining plum mixture. Garnish with a cookie, dollop of whipped cream and plum slice if desired.

YIELD: 4 servings

Simple Pudding Pointer

When preparing a dessert that calls for instant pudding mix, avoid replacing it with a sugar-free variety. Lighter puddings don't set up like regular puddings and offer the dish less bulk.

SUMMER MELON PARFAITS

Taste of Home Test Kitchen

"This cool dessert will surely refresh you and your family in the heat of summer. Even kids who don't care for fruit will gobble up this treat."

PREP/TOTAL TIME: 15 minutes

1/4	cup lemonade concentrate
1/4	cup lemon, orange *or* raspberry yogurt
1	carton (8 ounces) frozen whipped topping, thawed
1	cup diced honeydew
1	cup diced cantaloupe

In a large bowl, combine lemonade concentrate and yogurt; fold in whipped topping. In each of four dessert glasses, layer 1/4 cup honeydew, 1/4 cup lemon mixture, 1/4 cup cantaloupe and remaining lemon mixture.

YIELD: 4 servings

LIGHT LEMON MOUSSE

Joan Jay ● FRISCO, TEXAS

"This smooth, citrusy mousse is popular at cookouts, but it makes a delicious, light finish to hearty winter meals, too. For a pretty presentation, I serve it in individual glass dishes garnished with sliced fresh strawberries."

PREP: 20 minutes + chilling

3/4	cup sugar
1/2	cup cornstarch
3	cups fat-free milk
2/3	cup lemon juice
1-1/2	teaspoons grated lemon peel
1/4	teaspoon vanilla extract
2	cups reduced-fat whipped topping
3	drops yellow food coloring, optional

In a large saucepan, combine the sugar and cornstarch; gradually stir in milk until smooth. Bring to a boil over medium heat, stirring constantly. Cook and stir for 2 minutes or until thickened and bubbly. Remove from the heat. Stir in the lemon juice, peel and vanilla.

Set saucepan in ice; stir until mixture reaches room temperature, about 5 minutes. Fold in whipped topping and food coloring if desired. Spoon into dessert dishes. Refrigerate for at least 1 hour before serving.

YIELD: 10 servings

S'MORE PARFAITS

Vonnie Oyer ● HUBBARD, OREGON

"Our son Jason loves s'mores and parfait desserts, so we combined them to create these snacks. Crushed graham crackers, chocolate pudding, mini marshmallows and chips are layered into tall glasses for a fun look."

PREP: 10 minutes + chilling

2	cups cold milk
1	package (3.9 ounces) instant chocolate fudge *or* chocolate pudding mix
2	cups coarsely crushed graham crackers (about 24 squares)
1	cup miniature marshmallows
4	tablespoons miniature semisweet chocolate chips

In a bowl, whisk milk and pudding mix for 2 minutes. Let stand for 2 minutes or until soft-set. Spoon 3 tablespoons each into four parfait glasses. Layer each with 1/4 cup cracker crumbs, 3 tablespoons pudding, 1/4 cup marshmallows and 1 tablespoon chocolate chips. Top with the remaining pudding and crumbs. Refrigerate for 1 hour before serving.

YIELD: 4 servings

VERY BERRY PARFAITS

Andree Garrett
PLYMOUTH, MICHIGAN

"When I asked drop-in company to stay for dinner, I had all the ingredients on hand to create this elegant, layered berry treat."

PREP: 15 minutes + chilling

- 1 package (.3 ounce) sugar-free strawberry gelatin
- 1 cup boiling water
- 1 cup cold water
- 2 cups fresh *or* frozen blueberries, *divided*
- 2 cups sliced fresh *or* frozen unsweetened strawberries, *divided*
- 1-3/4 cups cold fat-free milk
- 1 package (1 ounce) sugar-free instant vanilla pudding mix

In a large bowl, dissolve gelatin in boiling water. Stir in cold water. Pour into eight parfait glasses; refrigerate until firm, about 1 hour.

Top with half of the blueberries and half of the strawberries. In a large bowl, whisk milk and pudding mix for 2 minutes. Let stand for 2 minutes or until soft-set. Pour over berries. Top with remaining berries. Cover and refrigerate 1 hour longer.

YIELD: 8 servings

81

PEANUT BUTTER BANANA PUDDING

Laura McGinnis ● COLORADO SPRINGS, COLORADO

"If there's anything I like better than bananas, it's bananas with peanut butter!"

PREP/TOTAL TIME: 20 minutes

      4   cups milk
      1   package (3 ounces) vanilla
          cook-and-serve pudding mix
      1   package (3-1/2 ounces)
          butterscotch cook-and-serve
          pudding mix
  1-1/2   cups peanut butter, *divided*
      1   cup graham cracker crumbs
      1   cup confectioners' sugar
      4   medium firm bananas, sliced

In a large saucepan, combine milk and pudding mixes until blended. Bring to a boil over medium heat, stirring constantly. Remove from the heat; stir in 1/2 cup peanut butter until blended. Cover and refrigerate until chilled.

Meanwhile, in a small bowl, combine cracker crumbs and confectioners' sugar; cut in remaining peanut butter until crumbly.

In individual dessert bowls, layer half of the pudding, half of the crumb mixture and half of the bananas. Repeat the layers.

YIELD: 12 servings

MELON MOUSSE

Sandra McKenzie ● BRAHAM, MINNESOTA

"This unique summer dessert is low in fat and a creative way to use cantaloupe. It's best when made with very ripe melon to give the sweetest flavor."

PREP: 15 minutes + chilling

  2   envelopes unflavored gelatin
  3   tablespoons lemon juice
  4   cups cubed ripe cantaloupe
  1   tablespoon sugar
  1   carton (8 ounces) fat-free lemon
      yogurt
Fresh raspberries, optional

In a small saucepan, sprinkle gelatin over lemon juice; let stand for 1 minute. Heat over low heat, stirring until gelatin is completely dissolved.

In a blender, combine the gelatin mixture, cantaloupe and sugar; cover and process until smooth. Transfer to a bowl; stir in yogurt. Spoon into individual dishes; chill until firm. Garnish with raspberries if desired.

YIELD: 6 servings

WALNUT PUDDING

Peggy Foster ● LA PLATA, MISSOURI

"My grandmother always made this pudding for holiday gatherings...my mother served it to us often as we were growing up."

PREP: 15 minutes + chilling

  1/2   cup sugar
  1/4   cup all-purpose flour
  1/2   teaspoon baking soda
    2   cups warm milk (120°)
  1/2   cup chopped walnuts
Whipped cream and additional walnuts,
    optional

In a small heavy skillet, combine sugar, flour and baking soda; cook and stir over medium heat until light brown. Reduce heat to low; gradually stir in milk. Cook and stir until thickened and bubbly. Stir in nuts. Pour into two serving dishes. Chill. Garnish with whipped cream and walnuts if desired.

YIELD: 2 servings

CRANBERRY FOOL

Taste of Home Test Kitchen

"A 'fool' is a dessert made by folding pureed fruit into whipped cream. In this delectable version, cranberry sauce is the featured fruit."

PREP: 10 minutes + chilling

1 can (16 ounces) whole-berry cranberry sauce
1 teaspoon grated orange peel
1/4 teaspoon ground allspice
1 cup heavy whipping cream, whipped

Additional grated orange peel, optional
Fresh mint, optional

In a bowl, combine the cranberry sauce, orange peel and allspice. Fold in whipped cream. Spoon into dishes. Refrigerate until serving. Garnish with orange peel and mint if desired.

YIELD: 4 servings

LAYERED BANANA PUDDING

Esther Matteson • BREMEN, INDIANA

"My mother gave me this recipe, which an old friend had shared with her. When my children were still at home, we enjoyed this satisfying pudding."

PREP: 30 minutes + chilling

1/2 cup all-purpose flour
2/3 cup packed brown sugar
2 cups milk
2 egg yolks, beaten
2 tablespoons butter
1 teaspoon vanilla extract
1 cup heavy whipping cream, whipped
4 to 6 medium firm bananas, sliced

Chopped walnuts, optional

In a large saucepan, combine the flour and brown sugar. Stir in milk until smooth. Cook and stir over medium-high heat until thickened and bubbly. Reduce heat; cook and stir 2 minutes longer. Remove from the heat.

Stir a small amount of hot filling into egg yolks; return all to pan, stirring constantly. Bring to a gentle boil; cook and stir 2 minutes longer. Remove from the heat; stir in butter and vanilla. Cool to room temperature without stirring. Fold in the whipped cream.

Layer a third of the pudding in a 2-qt. glass bowl; top with half of the bananas. Repeat layers. Top with remaining pudding. Sprinkle with nuts if desired. Cover and refrigerate for at least 1 hour before serving.

YIELD: 8 servings

BLACK CHERRY CREAM PARFAITS

Margaret Schmieder • SPARKS, NEVADA

"This dessert is light and cool but incredibly decadent-tasting."

PREP: 15 minutes + chilling

2 packages (3 ounces *each*) black cherry gelatin
2 cups boiling water
2 cups black cherry soda, chilled
1 cup heavy whipping cream
1/2 cup confectioners' sugar
1 can (15 ounces) pitted dark sweet cherries, drained
1/2 cup chopped walnuts

In a large bowl, dissolve gelatin in boiling water. Stir in soda; refrigerate for 2 hours or until partially set.

In a large mixing bowl, beat cream until it begins to thicken. Add confectioners' sugar; beat until soft peaks form. Stir cherries and walnuts into gelatin; fold in whipped cream. Spoon into parfait glasses. Chill until firm.

YIELD: 10 servings

APRICOT RICE CUSTARD

Elizabeth Montgomery
TAYLORVILLE, ILLINOIS

"Creamy rice custard drizzled with apricot sauce makes a comforting dessert or even breakfast."

PREP: 35 minutes
COOK: 15 minutes + chilling

- 1 cup uncooked long grain rice
- 3 cups milk
- 1/2 cup sugar
- 1/2 teaspoon salt
- 2 eggs, lightly beaten
- 1/2 teaspoon vanilla extract
- 1/4 teaspoon almond extract

Dash ground cinnamon

SAUCE:

- 1 can (8-1/2 ounces) apricot halves
- 1 can (8 ounces) crushed pineapple, undrained
- 1/3 cup packed brown sugar
- 2 tablespoons lemon juice
- 1 tablespoon cornstarch

In a large saucepan, cook rice according to package directions. Stir in milk, sugar and salt; bring to a boil. Reduce heat to low. Stir 1/2 cup into eggs; return all to the pan, stirring constantly. Cook and stir for 15 minutes or until mixture reaches 160° and coats the back of a metal spoon (do not boil). Remove from the heat; stir in extracts and cinnamon.

For sauce, drain apricot syrup into a small saucepan. Chop apricots; add to syrup. Stir in remaining sauce ingredients; bring to a boil. Boil for 2 minutes, stirring occasionally. Refrigerate sauce and custard until serving.

YIELD: 8-10 servings

RASPBERRY CHOCOLATE TRIFLE

Taste of Home Test Kitchen

"Elegant but easy perfectly describes this rich trifle. Prepared pound cake and frozen berries create the mouth-watering masterpiece."

PREP: 15 minutes + chilling

- 2 cups cold milk
- 1 package (3.9 ounces) instant chocolate pudding mix
- 1 loaf (10-3/4 ounces) frozen pound cake, thawed
- 2 cups fresh *or* frozen raspberries, thawed
- 1 cup raspberry preserves

Whipped topping

Additional raspberries, optional

Mix milk and pudding mix according to package directions; chill. Cut cake into 1-in. cubes; place half in a 2-qt. glass bowl. In a small bowl, gently stir together raspberries and preserves; spoon half over cake.

Pour half of the pudding over raspberries. Cover with remaining cake cubes. Layer with remaining berries and pudding. Chill until serving. Garnish with whipped topping and raspberries if desired.

YIELD: 4-6 servings

HEAVENLY CHOCOLATE MOUSSE

Christy Freeman • CENTRAL POINT, OREGON

"One friend describes my chocolaty dessert as heaven on a spoon."

PREP: 30 minutes + chilling

- 8 squares (1 ounce *each*) semisweet chocolate, coarsely chopped
- 1/2 cup water, *divided*
- 2 tablespoons butter
- 3 egg yolks
- 2 tablespoons sugar
- 1-1/4 cups heavy whipping cream, whipped

In a microwave, microwave the chocolate, 1/4 cup water and butter until the chocolate and butter are melted; stir until smooth. Cool for 10 minutes.

In a small heavy saucepan, whisk egg yolks, sugar and remaining water. Cook and stir over medium heat until mixture reaches 160° and is thick enough to coat the back of a metal spoon. Remove from the heat; whisk in chocolate mixture.

Set saucepan in ice and stir until cooled, about 5-10 minutes. Fold in the whipped cream. Spoon into dessert dishes. Refrigerate for 4 hours or overnight.

YIELD: 6-8 servings

PUMPKIN CRUNCH PARFAITS

Lorraine Darocha • BERKSHIRE, MASSACHUSETTS

"Here's a fun treat that youngsters can help prepare."

PREP/TOTAL TIME: 15 minutes

- 3/4 cup cold milk
- 1 package (3.4 ounces) instant vanilla pudding mix
- 2 cups whipped topping
- 1 cup canned pumpkin
- 1/2 teaspoon pumpkin pie spice
- 1 cup chopped pecans
- 32 gingersnap cookies, crushed (about 1-1/2 cups)

Additional whipped topping

In a large mixing bowl, beat milk and pudding mix on low speed for 2 minutes. Stir in the whipped topping, pumpkin and pumpkin pie spice. Fold in pecans.

Spoon half of the mixture into parfait glasses; top with half of the gingersnap crumbs. Repeat layers. Top with additional whipped topping.

YIELD: 6 servings

STRAWBERRY TIRAMISU TRIFLE

Tammy Irvine ● WHITBY, ONTARIO

"We do a lot of entertaining. I like to make this easy trifle when I want to impress people. Berries make it different from a traditional tiramisu."

PREP: 30 minutes + chilling

- 1 **quart fresh strawberries**
- 1-1/4 **cups cold milk**
- 1 **package (3.4 ounces) instant vanilla pudding mix**
- 1 **package (8 ounces) cream cheese, softened**
- 4 **tablespoons strong brewed coffee, room temperature, *divided***
- 2 **cups whipped topping**
- 1 **package (3 ounces) ladyfingers, split**
- 6 **squares (1 ounce *each*) bittersweet chocolate, grated**

Set aside three strawberries for garnish; slice the remaining strawberries. In a bowl, whisk milk and pudding mix for 2 minutes. Let stand for 2 minutes or until soft-set. In a large mixing bowl, beat cream cheese until smooth; gradually beat in 2 tablespoons coffee. Beat in pudding. Fold in whipped topping.

Brush remaining coffee over ladyfingers. Line the bottom of a 3-qt. trifle or glass serving bowl with half of the ladyfingers. Top with half of the sliced berries, grated chocolate and pudding mixture; repeat layers. Cut reserved berries in half; place on trifle. Cover and refrigerate for 4 hours or overnight.

YIELD: 12 servings

RHUBARB GINGERSNAP PARFAITS

Diane Halferty ● CORPUS CHRISTI, TEXAS

"I created this recipe to showcase one of my favorite garden plants—rhubarb. My four children are grown, but I enjoy fixing this colorful dessert for my grandchildren."

PREP: 20 minutes + chilling COOK: 15 minutes + cooling

- 4 **cups chopped fresh *or* frozen rhubarb (about 1 pound)**
- 1/2 **cup sugar**
- 3/4 **cup heavy whipping cream**
- 3 **tablespoons confectioners' sugar**
- 1/3 **cup sour cream**
- 1/8 **teaspoon almond extract**
- 2 **tablespoons coarsely crushed gingersnaps**

In a large saucepan, bring rhubarb and sugar to a boil over medium heat, stirring constantly. Reduce heat; simmer, uncovered, until rhubarb is tender and mixture is reduced to 1-1/3 cups. Remove from the heat. Cool for 30 minutes. Cover and refrigerate.

In a large mixing bowl, beat the whipping cream until soft peaks form. Beat in confectioners' sugar. Add sour cream and extract; beat until stiff peaks form.

In four parfait glasses, place about 2 tablespoons rhubarb mixture and 1/4 cup cream mixture; repeat layers. Sprinkle with gingersnaps. Chill until serving.

YIELD: 4 servings

Editor's Note: If using frozen rhubarb, measure rhubarb while still frozen, then thaw completely. Drain in a colander, but do not press liquid out.

PUMPKIN MOUSSE

Taste of Home Test Kitchen

"If you've had your fill of pumpkin pie, this cool and creamy mousse is just right for you. Its light and fluffy texture won't make you feel 'stuffed' after your favorite turkey dinner."

PREP: 10 minutes + chilling

1	package (8 ounces) cream cheese, softened
1/4	cup sugar
1	can (15 ounces) solid-pack pumpkin
1	package (3.4 ounces) instant vanilla pudding mix
2	teaspoons pumpkin pie spice
1	cup cold milk
1	carton (4 ounces) frozen whipped topping, thawed
24	gingersnaps

In a large mixing bowl, beat cream cheese and sugar until smooth. Beat in pumpkin. Add pudding mix and pie spice until blended. Gradually beat in milk. Fold in whipped topping.

Spoon about 1/4 cup each into serving dishes. Crumble 2 gingersnaps over each. Divide remaining pumpkin mixture among dishes. Garnish with a whole gingersnap. Chill until serving.

YIELD: 8 servings

ANGEL BERRY TRIFLE

Brenda Paine ● CLINTON TOWNSHIP, MICHIGAN

"I usually serve this heart-smart sensation in the summertime when fresh berries are bountiful. I once prepared it, however, using frozen cherries and a can of light cherry pie filling instead. It was an absolutely delicious glimpse of the wonderful summer flavors that were to come!"

PREP/TOTAL TIME: 15 minutes

1-1/2	cups cold fat-free milk
1	package (1 ounce) sugar-free instant vanilla pudding mix
1	cup (8 ounces) fat-free vanilla yogurt
6	ounces reduced-fat cream cheese, cubed
1/2	cup reduced-fat sour cream
2	teaspoons vanilla extract
1	carton (12 ounces) frozen reduced-fat whipped topping, thawed, *divided*
1	prepared angel food cake (18 inches), cut into 1-inch cubes
1	pint *each* blackberries, raspberries and blueberries

In a small bowl, whisk the milk and pudding mix for 2 minutes or until thickened. In a mixing bowl, beat the yogurt, cream cheese, sour cream and vanilla until smooth. Fold in pudding mixture and 1 cup whipped topping.

Place a third of the cake cubes in a 4-qt. trifle bowl. Top with a third of the pudding mixture, a third of the berries and half of the remaining whipped topping. Repeat layers once. Top with the remaining cake cubes, pudding and berries. Serve trifle immediately or refrigerate.

YIELD: 14 servings

Dressed-Up Desserts

It's a snap to jazz up leftover birthday cake, extra brownies or even day-old coffee cake! Simply layer cubes of the dessert in a bowl with your favorite flavor of pudding or whipped topping.

CHOCOLATE 'N' TOFFEE RICE PUDDING

Joann Vess Hilliard ● EAST LIVERPOOL, OHIO

"I can't think of a more comforting dessert than this pudding."

PREP: 10 minutes COOK: 15 minutes + chilling

3	cups milk
3	cups cooked rice
1/2	cup packed brown sugar
3	tablespoons butter
1/4	teaspoon salt
1	teaspoon vanilla extract
1/4	cup flaked coconut, toasted
1/4	cup English toffee bits *or* almond brickle chips
1/4	cup miniature semisweet chocolate chips
1/2	cup whipped topping
7	maraschino cherries

In a large saucepan, combine the milk, rice, brown sugar, butter and salt; bring to a boil over medium heat. Cook for 15 minutes or until thick and creamy, stirring occasionally. Remove from the heat; stir in vanilla. Cool.

Spoon half of the pudding into dessert dishes. Combine the coconut, toffee bits and chocolate chips; sprinkle half over the pudding. Repeat layers. Refrigerate until serving. Top with whipped topping and cherries.

YIELD: 7 servings

PARADISE PARFAITS

Lee Ann Odell ● ERIE, COLORADO

"This is a favorite with my gang. Cookie crumbs and coconut add a fun twist."

PREP/TOTAL TIME: 15 minutes

2	cups cold fat-free milk
1	package (3.4 ounces) instant French vanilla pudding mix
1/4	teaspoon coconut extract
16	reduced-fat vanilla wafers, *divided*
1	medium firm banana, sliced
4	tablespoons chopped walnuts, toasted
1	cup sliced fresh strawberries
3/4	cup halved green grapes
2	tablespoons flaked coconut, toasted

In a bowl, whisk milk and pudding mix for 2 minutes. Whisk in extract. Let stand for 2 minutes or until soft-set. Refrigerate for 5 minutes.

Coarsely crush 12 wafers. In glasses, layer banana, half of the cookie crumbs, nuts and pudding, and all of the berries. Top with the remaining cookie crumbs and pudding, all of the grapes and remaining nuts. Garnish with toasted coconut and a whole vanilla wafer.

YIELD: 4 servings

COCONUT PARFAITS

Merval Harvey ● GLENNIE, MICHIGAN

"Every time I serve this to guests, I have to give them the recipe, too."

PREP: 15 minutes + freezing COOK: 5 minutes + cooling

6	tablespoons water
3	tablespoons sugar
1/2	cup flaked coconut
1-1/2	teaspoons vanilla extract
1/2	cup heavy whipping cream
1	tablespoon sliced almonds, toasted
1	tablespoon flaked coconut, toasted

In a saucepan, combine water and sugar. Bring to a boil over medium heat; boil for 5 minutes. Remove from heat; cool for 10 minutes. Stir in coconut and vanilla. Cool to room temperature.

In a mixing bowl, beat cream until soft peaks form; fold into coconut mixture. Pour into dishes. Freeze 1 hour or overnight. Before serving, sprinkle with almonds and toasted coconut.

YIELD: 2 servings

WHITE CHOCOLATE CHERRY PARFAITS

Rita Sherman
COLEVILLE, CALIFORNIA

"Layers of silky mousse and sweet cherry sauce with a hint of orange alternate in this delectable dessert."

PREP: 40 minutes + chilling

- 1/2 cup sugar
- 2 tablespoons cornstarch
- 1/2 cup water
- 2 cups fresh *or* frozen pitted tart cherries
- 1/2 teaspoon orange extract

WHITE CHOCOLATE MOUSSE:

- 3 tablespoons sugar
- 1 teaspoon cornstarch
- 1/2 cup milk
- 2 egg yolks, lightly beaten
- 4 squares (1 ounce *each*) white baking chocolate, chopped
- 1/2 teaspoon vanilla extract
- 1-1/2 cups heavy whipping cream, whipped

In a saucepan, combine sugar and cornstarch; stir in water until smooth. Add cherries. Bring to a boil over medium heat; cook and stir for 2 minutes or until thickened. Remove from heat; stir in extract. Refrigerate until chilled.

In another saucepan, combine the sugar and cornstarch; stir in milk until smooth. Bring to a boil over medium heat. Reduce heat; cook and stir for 2 minutes. Remove from heat. Whisk a small amount of hot filling into egg yolks; return all to the pan, whisking constantly. Bring to a gentle boil; cook and stir for 2 minutes. Remove from the heat. Stir in chocolate and vanilla until chocolate is melted. Cool to room temperature. Fold in whipped cream.

Spoon 1/4 cup mousse into each glass. Top with a rounded 1/4 cup of cherry mixture. Repeat layers. Refrigerate until chilled.

YIELD: 6 servings

MARSHMALLOW CREAM WITH CUSTARD SAUCE

Penny Klusman ● RICHMOND, INDIANA

"This dessert has always been a favorite of my husband and children. The original recipe came from my great-grandmother and has been passed down through the generations. It's special enough for festive occasions year-round."

PREP: 25 minutes + chilling COOK: 20 minutes

> 2   egg whites
> 1/4 cup sugar
> **Pinch salt**
> 1/4 teaspoon vanilla extract
> **CUSTARD SAUCE:**
> 1-1/2 cups milk
> 2   egg yolks
> 1   egg
> 1/4 cup sugar
> 2   teaspoons vanilla extract
> **Fresh raspberries**

In a small heavy saucepan, combine the egg whites, sugar, salt and vanilla. Beat with a portable mixer on high speed until mixture reaches 160°. Beat until stiff peaks form, about 1 minute.

Spoon into dessert glasses; refrigerate until chilled.

For the custard sauce, heat milk in a small saucepan over medium heat until small bubbles form around side of pan. Remove from heat. Combine egg yolks, egg and sugar in a bowl. Whisk a small amount of hot milk into egg mixture; return all to pan, whisking constantly. Cook and stir on low until mixture reaches 160° and coats a spoon, about 20 minutes. Remove from the heat; stir in vanilla. Refrigerate for at least 1 hour.

Serve custard over marshmallow cream; top with raspberries.

YIELD: 6 servings

CHERRY TRIFLE

Margo Seegrist ● SHELTON, WASHINGTON

"The chocolate syrup in this tempting trifle is a sweet surprise. Everyone loves the topping of the toasted coconut and almonds."

PREP: 20 minutes + chilling

> 2-1/4 cups cold milk, *divided*
> 1   package (3.4 ounces) instant vanilla pudding mix
> 1   envelope whipped topping mix
> 1/2 teaspoon vanilla extract
> 1   prepared angel food cake (10 inches)
> 2   tablespoons maraschino cherry juice, *divided*
> 1   can (21 ounces) cherry pie filling
> 3/4 cup chocolate syrup, *divided*
> 1/2 cup flaked coconut, toasted
> 1/4 cup sliced almonds, toasted

In a large mixing bowl, combine 1-3/4 cups of milk and pudding mix. Beat on low speed for 2 minutes. Let stand for 2 minutes or until soft-set. In another large mixing bowl, beat the whipped topping mix, vanilla and remaining milk until stiff peaks form.

Cut cake into 1/2-in. cubes; place half in a 3-qt. glass bowl. Sprinkle with 1 tablespoon cherry juice. Top with half of the pie filling, half of the pudding and 1/4 cup of chocolate syrup. Repeat layers. Top with whipped topping and remaining syrup. Sprinkle with coconut and almonds. Cover and refrigerate for at least 4 hours.

YIELD: 12-15 servings

RASPBERRY RICE PUDDING

Shirley Privratsky ● Dickinson, North Dakota

"This is one of my family's most-requested desserts. It's so festive looking, especially when served in a clear glass bowl or topped with raspberries."

PREP: 5 minutes COOK: 35 minutes + chilling

- 2 cups water
- 1 cup long grain rice
- 3 cups milk
- 3/4 to 1 cup sugar
- 1 carton (8 ounces) frozen whipped topping, thawed
- 2 packages (10 ounces *each*) frozen raspberries, thawed
- 2 tablespoons cornstarch

In a large saucepan, bring water to a boil. Stir in rice. Reduce heat; cover and simmer for 10 minutes, stirring occasionally. Stir in milk and sugar. Cook 20-30 minutes longer or until rice is tender and mixture is thick and creamy. Remove from the heat; cool. Fold in whipped topping. Chill.

Drain raspberries, reserving juice. In a small saucepan, combine the cornstarch and reserved juice until smooth. Bring to a boil; cook and stir for 2 minutes or until thickened. Stir in raspberries. Remove from the heat; cool.

Spoon the rice pudding into individual dishes; top with the raspberry mixture. Cover and refrigerate until serving.

YIELD: 10-12 servings

COFFEE MOUSSE

Vernette Dechaine ● Pittsfield, Maine

"The recipe for this low-sugar treat comes from my daughter. Its texture is light as a cloud and its taste is perfect for coffee lovers."

PREP: 15 minutes + chilling

- 1 envelope unflavored gelatin
- 1/4 cup cold water
- 2 teaspoons instant coffee granules
- 1/4 cup boiling water

Sugar substitute equivalent to 2 teaspoons sugar

- 2 ice cubes
- 2 cups plus 4 tablespoons reduced-fat whipped topping, *divided*

Additional coffee granules, crushed

In a small bowl, sprinkle gelatin over cold water; let stand for 2 minutes. In a small saucepan, dissolve coffee granules in boiling water. Add gelatin mixture; cook and stir just until gelatin is dissolved (do not boil).

Remove from the heat; stir in sugar substitute. Add ice cubes; stir until ice is melted and mixture begins to thicken. Transfer to a mixing bowl; add 2/3 cup whipped topping. Beat until blended. Fold in 1-1/3 cups whipped topping.

Spoon into four individual serving dishes; top each with 1 tablespoon whipped topping. Refrigerate for at least 2 hours. Just before serving, dust with crushed coffee granules.

YIELD: 4 servings

Editor's Note: This recipe was tested with Splenda No Calorie Sweetener.

CHAPTER 5
Company's Coming

Black Forest Freezer Pie, 96

INDIVIDUAL CRANBERRY TRIFLES

Taste of Home Test Kitchen

"If you don't have enough individual parfaits, you can make this dessert in a trifle bowl. Either way, it's sure to bring you rave reviews."

PREP: 45 minutes + chilling

1 package (16 ounces) angel food cake mix
2 packages (8 ounces *each*) cream cheese, softened
2 cups confectioners' sugar
1 cup (8 ounces) sour cream
1 teaspoon vanilla extract
1 carton (12 ounces) frozen whipped topping, thawed
2 cans (16 ounces *each*) whole-berry cranberry sauce
2 tablespoons sugar
2 to 3 teaspoons grated orange peel
Fresh cranberrles *or* mint, optional

Prepare, bake and cool angel food cake according to package directions. Cut into 1-in. cubes; set aside. In a large mixing bowl, combine cream cheese, confectioners' sugar, sour cream and vanilla; beat until smooth. Fold in whipped topping. In a bowl, combine the cranberry sauce, sugar and orange peel.

In individual parfait glasses or a 3-qt. trifle bowl, layer half of the cake cubes, cranberry mixture and whipped topping mixture. Repeat layers. Refrigerate until serving. Garnish with cranberries and mint if desired.

YIELD: 14-16 servings

COLOSSAL CARAMEL APPLE TRIFLE

Deborah Randall ● ABBEVILLE, LOUISIANA

"As a pastor's wife and state auxiliary leader, I host many large gatherings. Whenever I make this 'punch bowl cake,' it makes a big impression, and I return with an empty bowl every time!"

PREP: 40 minutes + chilling

1 package (18-1/4 ounces) yellow cake mix
6 cups cold milk
3 packages (3.4 ounces *each*) instant vanilla pudding mix
1 teaspoon apple pie spice
1 jar (12-1/4 ounces) caramel ice cream topping
1-1/2 cups chopped pecans, toasted
2 cans (21 ounces *each*) apple pie filling
2 cartons (16 ounces *each*) frozen whipped topping, thawed

Prepare and bake cake according to package directions, using two greased 9-in. round baking pans. Cool for 10 minutes before removing to wire racks to cool completely.

In a large bowl, whisk milk, pudding

mixes and apple pie spice for 2 minutes. Let stand for 2 minutes or until soft-set.

Cut one cake layer if necessary to fit evenly in an 8-qt. punch bowl. Poke holes in cake with a long wooden skewer; gradually pour a third of the caramel topping over cake. Sprinkle with 1/2 cup pecans and spread with half of the pudding mixture.

Spoon one can of pie filling over pudding; spread with one carton of whipped topping. Top with remaining cake and repeat layers. Drizzle with remaining caramel topping and sprinkle with remaining pecans. Refrigerate until serving.

YIELD: 42 servings

MOCHA ALMOND DESSERT

Taste of Home Test Kitchen

"For an easy, make-ahead dessert that's elegant and luscious, try this recipe. The perfect blend of mocha and chocolate is in each cool, refreshing slice."

PREP: 20 minutes + freezing

1	cup cream-filled chocolate sandwich cookie crumbs
1/4	cup sugar
1/4	cup butter, melted
1	package (8 ounces) cream cheese, softened
1	can (14 ounces) sweetened condensed milk
2/3	cup chocolate syrup
1/2	teaspoon vanilla extract
2	tablespoons instant coffee granules
1	tablespoon hot water
1	cup whipped topping
1/3	cup chopped almonds, toasted

Chocolate-covered coffee beans, optional

In a small bowl, combine the cookie crumbs, sugar and butter. Press onto the bottom and 1 in. up the sides of a greased 9-in. springform pan; set aside.

In a large mixing bowl, beat cream cheese, milk, chocolate syrup and vanilla until smooth. Dissolve coffee granules in hot water; beat into cream cheese mixture. Fold in whipped topping and almonds. Pour over crust. Cover and freeze for 8 hours or overnight.

Remove from the freezer 10-15 minutes before serving. Carefully run a knife around edge of pan to loosen. Remove sides of pan. Garnish with coffee beans if desired.

YIELD: 10-12 servings

CRANBERRY PISTACHIO ICE CREAM CAKE

Quadelle Rose • SPRINGBROOK, ALBERTA

"Red cranberries and green pistachios in this ice cream cake delightfully showcase the colors of the holiday season. My family prefers this homemade ice cream cake to store-bought desserts."

PREP: 30 minutes + freezing

1-1/2	cups crushed chocolate cream-filled cookies
1/4	cup butter, melted
1-1/2	cups fresh *or* frozen cranberries, thawed
1/2	cup light corn syrup
1/3	cup sugar
1/3	cup water
6	cups vanilla ice cream, softened, *divided*
1/2	cup chopped pistachios, *divided*

In a small bowl, combine crushed cookies and butter; press onto the bottom of a greased 9-in. springform pan. Freeze for 1 hour or until firm.

In a small saucepan, combine the cranberries, corn syrup, sugar and water. Bring to a boil; cook over medium heat until the berries pop, about 10 minutes. Transfer to a blender; cover and process until smooth. Pour into a large bowl. Refrigerate for 30 minutes or until cooled, stirring occasionally.

Remove crust from freezer. Spread with half of the ice cream. Set aside 1/4 cup cranberry puree. Pour remaining puree over ice cream. Set aside 1 tablespoon nuts; sprinkle remaining nuts over puree. Freeze for 30 minutes or until firm.

Layer with remaining ice cream, puree and nuts. Cover with plastic wrap; freeze for 6 hours or until firm. Remove from freezer 15 minutes before serving.

YIELD: 8-12 servings

ORANGE CREAM CHEESECAKE

Madonna Faunce ● BOISE, IDAHO

"I love serving this impressive-looking cheesecake with its pretty layers and silky-smooth texture. The combination of orange gelatin, cream cheese and whipped topping is simply irresistible."

PREP: 25 minutes + chilling

- 2 cups graham cracker crumbs
- 1 teaspoon ground cinnamon
- 1 teaspoon grated orange peel
- 1/2 cup butter, melted

FILLING:
- 1 package (3 ounces) orange gelatin
- 3 packages (8 ounces *each*) cream cheese, softened
- 1-1/4 cups sugar
- 1 can (5 ounces) evaporated milk
- 1 teaspoon lemon juice
- 1/3 cup orange juice concentrate
- 1 teaspoon vanilla extract
- 1 envelope unflavored gelatin
- 2 tablespoons cold water
- 2 tablespoons boiling water
- 1 carton (8 ounces) frozen whipped topping, thawed

TOPPING:
- 2 cups whipped topping
- 1/4 cup sugar

Lemon slices, orange peel strips, kumquats and lemon balm for garnish, optional

In a large bowl, combine the cracker crumbs, cinnamon, orange peel and butter. Press onto the bottom of a greased 10-in. springform pan. Refrigerate for at least 30 minutes.

Prepare orange gelatin according to package directions. Set aside 1/2 cup at room temperature. Chill remaining gelatin until slightly thickened, about 40-60 minutes.

In a large mixing bowl, beat cream cheese and sugar for 2 minutes. Gradually beat in milk and lemon juice. Beat on medium-high speed 2 minutes longer. Gradually beat in orange juice concentrate and vanilla.

In a small bowl, sprinkle unflavored gelatin over cold water; let stand for 2 minutes. Stir in boiling water until gelatin is completely dissolved. Stir into room temperature orange gelatin. Stir into cream cheese mixture, then fold in whipped topping. Pour into crust.

For topping, in a large mixing bowl, beat whipped topping and sugar. Beat in refrigerated orange gelatin (mixture will be thin). Chill for 30 minutes. Gently spoon over filling (pan will be full). Refrigerate for 8 hours or overnight. Garnish with lemon slices, orange peel strips, kumquats and lemon balm if desired.

YIELD: 10-12 servings

TWO-TONE SHERBET TORTE

Kina Fink ● CROWN POINT, INDIANA

"I first prepared this beautiful dessert for a Fourth of July party. Ever since, my mom asks me to make it for just about every event we host."

PREP: 15 minutes + freezing

- 1-3/4 cups crushed gingersnaps (about 40 cookies)
- 1/4 cup butter, melted
- 4 cups lemon sherbet, softened
- 4 cups raspberry sherbet, softened
- 1 cup fresh raspberries
- 3 squares (1 ounce *each*) white chocolate

In a small bowl, combine the cookie crumbs and butter. Press into a greased 9-in. springform pan. Freeze

for 15 minutes. Wrap outside of pan in foil. Carefully spread lemon sherbet over crust; freeze for 30 minutes.

Top with raspberry sherbet; freeze for at least 1 hour. Before serving, sprinkle raspberries over the top. In a small microwave-safe bowl, microwave white chocolate at 30% power for 1-2 minutes or until melted; stir until smooth. Drizzle over berries.

YIELD: 10-12 servings

BLACK FOREST FREEZER PIE

Angie Helms • PONTOTOC, MISSISSIPPI

"A delightful dessert is never far off when you have this layered ice cream pie in the freezer. For variety, use strawberry pie filling and a chocolate crust."

PREP: 20 minutes + freezing

- 1 pint chocolate *or* vanilla ice cream, softened
- 1 extra-servings-size graham cracker crust (9 ounces)
- 4 ounces cream cheese, softened
- 1 cup confectioners' sugar
- 1 carton (8 ounces) frozen whipped topping, thawed
- 1 can (21 ounces) cherry pie filling, chilled
- 3 tablespoons chocolate syrup

Spoon ice cream into pie crust; cover and freeze for 15 minutes. Meanwhile, in a large mixing bowl, beat cream cheese and confectioners' sugar until smooth; fold in whipped topping. Set aside 1-1/2 cups for garnish.

Spread remaining cream cheese mixture over ice cream. Using the back of a spoon, make an 8-in.-diameter well in the center of the pie for the pie filling. Pipe reserved cream cheese mixture around pie.

Cover and freeze for 3-4 hours or until firm. May be frozen for up to 2 months. Just before serving, spoon pie filling into the well; drizzle with chocolate syrup. Serve immediately.

YIELD: 6-8 servings

CHOCOLATE MINT TORTE

Joni Mehl • GRAND RAPIDS, MICHIGAN

"This frozen treat comes together in a snap. I melt chocolate-covered mint candies and mix them into the creamy filling for refreshing flavor. A cookie-crumb crust and a sprinkling of extra mint candies make it fun any time of the year."

PREP: 35 minutes + freezing

- 27 cream-filled chocolate sandwich cookies, crushed
- 1/3 cup butter, melted
- 4 ounces chocolate-covered peppermint candies
- 1/4 cup milk
- 1 jar (7 ounces) marshmallow creme
- 2 cups heavy whipping cream, whipped

Additional whipped cream and chocolate-covered peppermint patties

In a small bowl, combine cookie crumbs and butter. Press onto the bottom and 1-1/2 in. up the sides of a greased 9-in. springform pan. Chill for at least 30 minutes.

In a small saucepan, heat candies and milk over low heat until candy is melted; stir until smooth. Cool for 10-15 minutes.

Place marshmallow creme in a large mixing bowl; gradually beat in mint mixture. Fold in whipped cream. Transfer to prepared crust. Cover and freeze until firm. May be frozen for up to 2 months.

Remove from the freezer about 30 minutes before serving. Remove sides of pan. Garnish with additional whipped cream and candies.

YIELD: 12 servings

Editor's Note: This recipe was tested with Junior Mints.

RASPBERRY WHITE CHOCOLATE MOUSSE

Mary Lou Wayman
SALT LAKE CITY, UTAH

"Raspberry sauce is an appealing base for this fluffy white chocolate mousse."

PREP: 25 minutes + chilling

1	package (10 ounces) frozen sweetened raspberries, thawed
2	tablespoons sugar
1	tablespoon frozen orange juice concentrate, thawed
2	cups heavy whipping cream
6	ounces white baking chocolate
1	teaspoon vanilla extract
1/4	cup milk chocolate chips
1	teaspoon vegetable oil

In a blender, combine the raspberries, sugar and orange juice concentrate; cover and process until smooth. Press through a sieve; discard seeds. Refrigerate sauce.

In a large saucepan, cook and stir cream and white chocolate over low heat until chocolate is melted. Stir in vanilla. Transfer to a large mixing bowl. Cover and refrigerate for 6 hours or until thickened, stirring occasionally.

Beat cream mixture on high speed until light and fluffy, about 1-1/2 minutes. Just before serving, melt chocolate chips and oil. Spoon 2 tablespoons of raspberry sauce on each plate. Pipe or spoon 1/2 cup chocolate mousse over sauce; drizzle with melted chocolate.

YIELD: 8 servings

CROWN JEWEL GELATIN PIE

Elaine Augustine • MANCHESTER, CONNECTICUT

"This colorful pie—an old family favorite—couldn't be easier for busy holiday cooks to make. The rich stained-glass look of gelatin cubes adds a festive note."

PREP: 15 minutes COOK: 10 minutes + chilling

1	package (3 ounces) raspberry gelatin
3	cups boiling water, *divided*
2	cups cold water, *divided*
1	package (3 ounces) lime gelatin
1	package (3 ounces) black cherry gelatin
1	cup pineapple juice
1/4	cup sugar
1	package (3 ounces) strawberry gelatin
1-1/2	cups heavy whipping cream
2	graham cracker crusts (9 inches)

In a small bowl, dissolve raspberry gelatin in 1 cup boiling water; stir in 1/2 cup cold water. Pour into a 9-in. x 5-in. x 3-in. loaf pan coated with cooking spray. Repeat with lime and black cherry gelatin, using two more loaf pans. Refrigerate until firm, about 2 hours. Cut each into 1/2-in. cubes.

In a saucepan, combine the pineapple juice and sugar. Bring to a boil. Add strawberry gelatin and stir until dissolved. Add remaining cold water. Transfer to a large bowl. Refrigerate until thickened but not firm, about 1-1/4 hours.

In a chilled mixing bowl, beat cream until soft peaks form. Fold whipped cream into strawberry gelatin mixture. Gently stir in cubed gelatin. Spoon mixture into crust. Refrigerate until firm, about 2 hours.

YIELD: 2 pies (6-8 servings each)

CHOCOLATE-CARAMEL SUPREME PIE

Diana Stewart • OELWEIN, IOWA

"At a church fund-raiser, I purchased a pie-a-month package furnished by a local family. From among all the varieties they made, this one was the best, with its chocolate crust, creamy caramel filling and fluffy topping."

PREP: 25 minutes + chilling

30	caramels
3	tablespoons butter, melted
2	tablespoons water
1	chocolate crumb crust (9 inches)
1/2	cup chopped pecans, toasted
1	package (3 ounces) cream cheese, softened
1/3	cup confectioners' sugar
3/4	cup milk chocolate chips
3	tablespoons hot water
1	carton (8 ounces) frozen whipped topping, thawed

Chocolate hearts *or* curls, optional

In a large saucepan, add the caramels, butter and water. Cook and stir over medium heat until caramels are melted. Spread over crust; sprinkle with pecans. Refrigerate for 1 hour.

In a large mixing bowl, beat cream cheese and sugar until smooth; spread over caramel layer. Refrigerate.

In a large saucepan, melt chocolate chips with hot water over low heat; stir until smooth. Cool slightly. Fold in whipped topping. Spread over cream cheese layer. Garnish with chocolate hearts or curls if desired. Chill until serving. Refrigerate leftovers.

YIELD: 8 servings

CHOCOLATE MOUSSE LOAF

Daphene Miller ● PRINCETON, MISSOURI

"This showstopping loaf would make a tempting centerpiece for the most sumptuous holiday table."

PREP: 15 minutes + chilling COOK: 15 minutes

2	cups heavy whipping cream, *divided*
3	egg yolks
16	squares (1 ounce *each*) semisweet baking chocolate
1/2	cup butter, cubed
1/2	cup light corn syrup
1/4	cup confectioners' sugar
1	teaspoon vanilla extract

RASPBERRY SAUCE:

1	package (10 ounces) frozen raspberries, thawed
1/4	cup light corn syrup

In a bowl, whisk 1/2 cup whipping cream and egg yolks; set aside. In a large saucepan, heat chocolate, butter and corn syrup over low heat until chocolate and butter are melted. Remove from the heat; stir about 1 cup into the egg yolk mixture. Return all to the pan. Cook and stir over medium heat until mixture reaches 160° and is thick enough to coat the back of a metal spoon. Remove from the heat and cool.

In a large mixing bowl, beat remaining cream until it begins to thicken. Add confectioners' sugar and vanilla; beat until soft peaks form. Fold into chocolate mixture.

Pour into a 9-in. x 5-in. x 3-in. loaf pan that has been lined with plastic wrap. Refrigerate for 8-10 hours.

For sauce, place raspberries in a blender; cover and puree. Strain and discard seeds. Stir corn syrup into raspberry puree; refrigerate. Unmold mousse onto a serving platter; serve with raspberry sauce.

YIELD: 12-14 servings

SWISS SWIRL ICE CREAM CAKE

Danielle Hales ● BALTIMORE, MARYLAND

"With cake rolls, ice cream and hot fudge, this dessert suits anyone with a sweet tooth. Family and friends get a kick out of this treat's fun appearance."

PREP: 30 minutes + freezing

10	to 12 Swiss cake rolls
2	pints vanilla ice cream, softened
3/4	cup hot fudge ice cream topping
2	pints chocolate ice cream, softened

Line a 2-qt. bowl with plastic wrap. Cut each cake roll into eight slices; place in prepared bowl, completely covering the bottom and sides. Cover and freeze for at least 20 minutes or until cake is firm.

Spread vanilla ice cream over cake. Cover and freeze for at least 1 hour. Spread with fudge topping. Freeze for at least 1 hour. Spread with chocolate ice cream. Cover and freeze for up to 2 months.

Just before serving, remove from the freezer and invert onto a serving plate. Remove bowl and plastic wrap. Cut into wedges.

YIELD: 12-14 servings

Editor's Note: This recipe was tested with Little Debbie Swiss Cake Rolls.

SNOWFLAKE PUDDING

Patricia Stratton
MUSKEGON, MICHIGAN

"Flakes of coconut give my pudding its snow-like texture—and plenty of tastes besides! The crimson currant-raspberry sauce is delicious and pretty, too."

PREP: 10 minutes
COOK: 10 minutes + chilling

1	envelope unflavored gelatin
1-1/4	cups cold milk, *divided*
1/2	cup sugar
1/2	teaspoon salt
1	teaspoon vanilla extract
1-1/3	cups flaked coconut, toasted
1	cup heavy whipping cream, whipped

SAUCE:

1	package (10 ounces) frozen sweetened raspberries, thawed
1-1/2	teaspoons cornstarch
1/2	cup red currant jelly

In a small saucepan, sprinkle gelatin over 1/4 cup milk; let stand for 1 minute. Heat over low heat, stirring until gelatin is completely dissolved.

In a large saucepan, combine the sugar, salt and remaining milk; heat just until sugar is dissolved. Remove from the heat; stir in gelatin mixture and vanilla. Refrigerate until partially set. Fold in coconut and whipped cream. Pour into dessert dishes or small bowls; refrigerate for at least 2 hours.

Meanwhile, strain raspberries to remove seeds. In a small saucepan, combine the cornstarch, raspberry pulp and currant jelly; stir until smooth. Bring to a boil; boil and stir for 2 minutes. Chill for at least 1 hour. Serve with pudding.

YIELD: 6 servings

CHRISTMAS CHEESECAKE

Verna Arthur • PERKINS, OKLAHOMA

"With a cheery cherry topping and mint green garnish, this is the perfect dessert to top off a holiday dinner."

PREP: 20 minutes + chilling COOK: 5 minutes

1-1/2	cups graham cracker crumbs (about 24 squares)
6	tablespoons butter, softened
1	envelope unflavored gelatin
1/4	cup cold water
1/4	cup milk
1	package (8 ounces) cream cheese, softened
1/2	cup confectioners' sugar
2	teaspoons grated lemon peel
1	carton (8 ounces) frozen whipped topping, thawed, *divided*
1	can (21 ounces) cherry pie filling

In a small bowl, combine crumbs and butter; press onto the bottom of a greased 9-in. springform pan. Chill 15 minutes.

In a small saucepan, combine gelatin and water; let stand for 1 minute. Add milk; cook and stir over low heat until gelatin is dissolved.

In a large mixing bowl, beat cream cheese and sugar until light and fluffy. Beat in gelatin mixture and lemon peel. Chill until partially set. Fold in 2 cups whipped topping. Pour over crust. Chill until firm, at least 3 hours. Spread pie filling over gelatin layer. Top with remaining whipped topping. Refrigerate leftovers.

YIELD: 10-12 servings

COOKIE ICE CREAM CAKE

Heather McKillip • AURORA, ILLINOIS

"I discovered this recipe on-line and changed it a little to suit my family's tastes. It always gets lots of compliments because people love the hot fudge topping and unique cookie crust. My husband says it's the best ice cream cake he's ever had."

PREP: 35 minutes + freezing

44	miniature chocolate chip cookies
1/4	cup butter, melted
1	cup hot fudge topping, *divided*
1	quart vanilla ice cream, softened
1	quart chocolate ice cream, softened

Crush 25 cookies; set remaining cookies aside. In a bowl, combine cookie crumbs and butter. Press onto the bottom of a greased 10-in. springform pan. Freeze for 15 minutes.

In a microwave-safe bowl, heat 3/4 cup hot fudge topping on high for 15-20 seconds or until pourable; spread over crust. Arrange reserved cookies around the edge of pan. Freeze for 15 minutes. Spread vanilla ice cream over fudge topping; freeze for 30 minutes. Spread with chocolate ice cream. Cover and freeze until firm. May be frozen for up to 2 months.

Remove from the freezer 10 minutes before serving. Remove sides of pan. Warm remaining hot fudge topping; drizzle over top.

YIELD: 10-12 servings

FROSTY GINGER PUMPKIN SQUARES

Kathryn Reeger • SHELOCTA, PENNSYLVANIA

"My family loves getting together to sample good food. While pumpkin makes it perfect for the holidays, this ice cream dessert is requested year-round."

PREP: 30 minutes + freezing

1/4	cup butter, melted
1	cup crushed graham crackers (about 16 squares)
1	cup crushed gingersnaps (about 18 cookies)
2	cups canned pumpkin
1	cup sugar
1/2	to 1 teaspoon ground cinnamon
1/2	teaspoon salt
1/2	teaspoon ground ginger
1/4	teaspoon ground nutmeg
1	cup chopped walnuts
1/2	gallon vanilla ice cream, softened slightly

In a large bowl, combine the butter and crushed graham crackers and gingersnaps. Press half of the crumb mixture into an ungreased 13-in. x 9-in. x 2-in. dish.

In a large bowl, combine the pumpkin, sugar, cinnamon, salt, ginger and nutmeg. Stir in walnuts. Fold in softened ice cream. Spoon into crust. Sprinkle remaining crumb mixture over top. Freeze until firm, about 3 hours.

YIELD: 12-15 servings

RED, WHITE AND BLUEBERRY PIE

Kimberly McFarland • BROKEN ARROW, OKLAHOMA

"This is a wonderful light dessert for a Fourth of July party or other summer get-together. And it's as pretty as it is tasty."

PREP: 30 minutes + chilling

4	squares (1 ounce *each*) white baking chocolate
8	whole fresh strawberries, halved lengthwise
1	reduced-fat graham cracker crust (8 inches)
3/4	cup sliced fresh strawberries
1	package (8 ounces) reduced-fat cream cheese, cubed
3/4	cup confectioners' sugar
3/4	cup cold fat-free milk
1	package (3.3 ounces) instant white chocolate pudding mix
1	cup fresh *or* frozen blueberries
1	cup reduced-fat whipped topping

In a microwave, melt white chocolate; stir until smooth. Dip the halved strawberries halfway in chocolate; allow excess to drip off. Place cut side down on a waxed paper-lined baking sheet. Refrigerate for 15 minutes or until set. Spread the remaining melted chocolate over the bottom and sides of crust. Arrange sliced strawberries in crust.

In a large mixing bowl, beat cream cheese and confectioners' sugar until smooth. Gradually add milk. Beat in pudding mix on low speed for 2 minutes or until thickened; spread evenly over sliced strawberries.

Place blueberries in center of pie. Arrange dipped strawberries around the edge. Pipe whipped topping between the strawberries and blueberries. Chill until serving.

YIELD: 8 servings

STRAWBERRY BANANA PIE

Bernice Janowski ● Stevens Point, Wisconsin

With its sugar-cone crust and layers of bananas and strawberry ice cream, this pretty pie never seems to last long...especially when our grandchildren visit. It's a favorite year-round, but we really enjoy it in summer, when fresh strawberries are plentiful.

Prep: 45 minutes + freezing

- 1 package (5-1/4 ounces) ice cream sugar cones, crushed
- 1/4 cup ground pecans
- 1/3 cup butter, melted
- 2 cups vanilla ice cream, softened
- 2 medium ripe bananas, mashed
- 2 large firm bananas, cut into 1/4-inch slices
- 2 cups strawberry ice cream, softened
- 1 pint fresh strawberries
- 1 carton (8 ounces) frozen whipped topping, thawed

In a bowl, combine the crushed ice cream cones, pecans and butter. Press onto the bottom and up the sides of a greased 10-in. pie plate. Refrigerate for at least 30 minutes.

In a bowl, combine vanilla ice cream and mashed bananas. Spread over the crust; cover and freeze for 30 minutes. Arrange sliced bananas over ice cream; cover and freeze for 30 minutes. Top with strawberry ice cream; cover and freeze for about 45 minutes.

Hull and halve strawberries; place around edge of pie. Mound or pipe whipped topping in center of pie. Cover and freeze for up to 1 month. Remove from the freezer about 30 minutes before serving.

Yield: 8-10 servings

CHOCOLATE PECAN ICE CREAM TORTE

Kelly Arvay ● Barberton, Ohio

This delectable dessert layers my favorite ice cream (chocolate) and my husband's favorite (butter pecan) on a shortbread crust, along with chocolate candy pieces, toasted pecans and caramel topping.

Prep: 20 minutes + freezing

- 1 jar (12-1/4 ounces) caramel ice cream topping
- 2 milk chocolate candy bars (1.55 ounces *each*), chopped
- 12 pecan shortbread cookies, crushed
- 3 tablespoons butter, melted
- 1 cup pecan halves, toasted, *divided*
- 1/2 gallon butter pecan ice cream, slightly softened
- 1/2 gallon chocolate ice cream, slightly softened

In a microwave-safe bowl, combine the caramel topping and candy bars. Microwave, uncovered, on high for 1-1/2 minutes or until candy bars are melted, stirring every 30 seconds. Cool.

In a small bowl, combine the cookie crumbs and butter. Press onto the bottom of a greased 10-in. springform pan. Chop 1/2 cup pecans; set aside. Spoon half of the butter pecan ice cream over crust. Drizzle with 2 tablespoons caramel sauce; sprinkle with 1/4 cup chopped pecans.

Spread half of the chocolate ice cream over top. Drizzle with 2 tablespoons caramel sauce; sprinkle with remaining chopped pecans.

Spoon remaining butter pecan ice cream around the edge of pan; spread remaining chocolate ice cream in center of pan. Cover and freeze overnight.

Carefully run a knife around edge of pan to loosen; remove sides of pan. Top with remaining pecan halves; drizzle with 2 tablespoons caramel sauce. Serve with remaining sauce.

Yield: 16-20 servings

PEPPERMINT ICE CREAM CAKE

Gloria Kaufmann • ORRVILLE, OHIO

"This is the kind of dessert that's perfect for any special occasion. What's also nice is the fact that the cake can be made a few days ahead and stored in the freezer until the celebration starts. It always looks fresh and tastes great."

PREP: 15 minutes + freezing

- **4 cups crisp rice cereal**
- **1 milk chocolate candy bar (7 ounces)**
- **1/2 cup butter, cubed**
- **1/2 gallon peppermint stick ice cream, softened**
- **2 cups whipped topping**
- **Peppermint candy canes *or* crushed peppermint candies**

Place cereal in a large bowl; set aside. Grate or shave 2 tablespoons of chocolate from candy bar; set aside. In a heavy saucepan, melt butter and remaining chocolate; stir until smooth. Pour over cereal and stir to coat. Press into the bottom of a greased 10-in. springform pan. Freeze for 30 minutes.

Spoon ice cream over crust. Freeze for 15 minutes. Spread with whipped topping; sprinkle with the shaved chocolate. Cover and freeze for several hours or overnight. Top with candy. Remove cake from freezer 5-10 minutes before serving. Remove sides of pan; cut with a sharp knife and serve immediately.

YIELD: 8-10 servings

LADYFINGER LEMON TORTE

Mrs. J. H. Carroll • OTTAWA, ONTARIO

"Golden ladyfingers frame the luscious custard filling of this lovely frozen dessert. Everyone enjoys the yummy combination of sweetness and lemony zest."

PREP: 30 minutes + freezing

- **5 egg yolks, lightly beaten**
- **1-1/2 cups sugar, *divided***
- **3/4 cup lemon juice**
- **2 egg whites**
- **1 tablespoon grated lemon peel**
- **2 cups heavy whipping cream**
- **2 packages (3 ounces *each*) ladyfingers, split**
- **Lemon peel and fresh mint leaves**

In a heavy saucepan, combine egg yolks, 1-1/4 cups sugar, lemon juice and egg whites. Bring to a boil over medium heat; cook and stir for 8-10 minutes or until mixture reaches 160° and is thick enough to coat a metal spoon. Remove from heat. Cool quickly by placing pan in a bowl of ice water; stir for 2 minutes. Stir in lemon peel. Transfer to a bowl; press plastic wrap onto surface of custard. Chill for 2-3 hours or until partially set.

In a large mixing bowl, beat cream on medium speed until soft peaks form. Gradually beat in remaining sugar, 1 tablespoon at a time, on high until stiff peaks form. Gradually fold whipped cream into the cooled lemon mixture.

Arrange 24 ladyfingers around edge of an ungreased 9-in. springform pan. Arrange 16 ladyfingers on bottom of pan. Spread with half of lemon mixture. Arrange remaining ladyfingers over lemon mixture; top with remaining lemon mixture.

Cover and freeze overnight. Remove from the freezer 5 minutes before cutting. Remove sides of the pan. Garnish with lemon peel and mint.

YIELD: 12 servings

CREAM CHEESE CLOUDS

Mary Ann Marino
WEST PITTSBURGH, PENNSYLVANIA

"This attractive dessert is like a meringue but without all the fuss. The 'clouds' are made the night before and quickly filled just before serving. In a pinch, I've used canned pie filling for the fresh strawberries."

PREP: 10 minutes + chilling

1	package (8 ounces) cream cheese, softened
3/4	cup confectioners' sugar
1/2	teaspoon vanilla extract
1	cup heavy whipping cream
2	quarts fresh strawberries, sliced
1	carton (8 ounces) frozen whipped topping, thawed

In a large mixing bowl, beat the cream cheese, sugar and vanilla until smooth. Gradually add cream, beating until thickened. Spoon mixture into 10 mounds on a waxed paper-lined baking sheet. Using the back of a spoon, shape into 3-in. cups. Freeze for 2 hours or overnight.

To serve, fill with strawberries and garnish with whipped topping.

YIELD: 10 servings

GENERAL RECIPE INDEX

*This handy index lists every recipe by food category and major ingredient,
so you can easily locate recipes to suit your needs.*

APPLES
Apple Cheesecake, 74
Apple Pie a la Mode, 44
Apple Pie Ice Cream, 34
Colossal Caramel Apple Trifle, 93

APRICOTS
Apricot Delight, 75
Apricot Peach Smoothies, 8
Apricot Rice Custard, 84

BANANAS
Banana Berry Drink, 10
Banana Berry Tarts, 73
Banana Cheesecake Dessert, 71
Banana Split Dessert, 34
Banana Split Smoothies, 13
Berry Banana Smoothies, 30
Blackberry Banana Smoothies, 22
Cherry Banana Cream Pie, 70
Chocolate Banana Smoothies, 16
Four-Fruit Smoothies, 22
Layered Banana Pudding, 83
Paradise Parfaits, 88
Peanut Butter Banana
    Pudding, 82
Strawberry Banana Dessert, 69
Strawberry Banana Pie, 103
Strawberry Banana Smoothies, 31
Three-Fruit Frozen Yogurt, 38
Tropical Milk Shakes, 6
Tropical Smoothies, 19

BLACKBERRIES
Angel Berry Trifle, 87
Berry Banana Smoothies, 30
Blackberry Banana Smoothies, 22
Blackberry Frozen Yogurt, 41
Blackberry Nectarine Pie, 57
Four-Berry Smoothies, 27
Very Berry Smoothies, 19

BLUEBERRIES
Angel Berry Trifle, 87
Berry Banana Smoothies, 30
Blueberry Angel Dessert, 60
Blueberry Cheesecake Ice
    Cream, 36
Blueberry Fruit Smoothies, 12
Blueberry Orange Smoothies, 26
Four-Berry Smoothies, 27
Lemon Blueberry Cheesecake, 70
Red, White and Blueberry Pie, 102
So-Healthy Smoothies, 26
Summer Berry Cheese Pie, 71
Two-Fruit Frosty, 14
Very Berry Parfaits, 81
Very Berry Smoothies, 19

CANTALOUPE
Cantaloupe Cooler, 8
Cantaloupe Sherbet, 45
Fruity Summer Cooler, 17
Melon Fruit Slush, 15
Melon Mousse, 82
Summer Melon Parfaits, 80

CARAMEL
Caramel-Pecan Cheese Pie, 59
Chocolate Caramel Supreme
    Pie, 98
Mini Caramel Cheesecakes, 67

CHEESECAKES
Apple Cheesecake, 74
Banana Cheesecake Dessert, 71
Christmas Cheesecake, 101
Lemon Blueberry Cheesecake, 70
Mini Caramel Cheesecakes, 67
No-Bake Chocolate Cheesecake, 68
Orange Cream Cheesecake, 95

CHERRIES
Black Cherry Cream Parfaits, 83

Black Forest Dessert, 60
Black Forest Freezer Pie, 96
Cherry Banana Cream Pie, 70
Cherry Berry Smoothies, 29
Cherry Cranberry Shakes, 31
Cherry Nut Ice Cream, 48
Cherry Trifle, 90
Cherry Yogurt Smoothies, 5
Christmas Cheesecake, 101
White Chocolate Cherry
    Parfaits, 89

CHOCOLATE
Black Forest Dessert, 60
Black Forest Freezer Pie, 96
Chocolate 'n' Toffee Rice
    Pudding, 88
Chocolate Banana Smoothies, 16
Chocolate-Caramel Supreme
    Pie, 98
Chocolate Cream Dessert, 74
Chocolate Cream Pie, 58
Chocolate Malted Ice Cream, 37
Chocolate Malts, 6
Chocolate Mint Eclair Dessert, 75
Chocolate Mint Torte, 96
Chocolate Mousse Loaf, 99
Chocolate Peanut Ice Cream
    Dessert, 51
Chocolate Pecan Ice Cream
    Torte, 103
Chocolate Raspberry Dessert, 38
Dark Chocolate Pudding, 78
Frozen Chocolate Crunch, 35
Frozen Mud Pie, 46
Fudgy Nut Coffee Pie, 52
Heavenly Chocolate Mousse, 85
Mint Chocolate Chip Pie, 49
No-Bake Chocolate Cheesecake, 68
Peppermint Chocolate Malt, 24
Raspberry Chocolate Trifle, 85

Pear Slushy, 19

PIES & TARTS
Frozen
Apple Pie a la Mode, 44
Black Forest Freezer Pie, 96
Frosty Freezer Pie, 33
Frosty Lemon Pie, 54
Frozen Mud Pie, 46
Fudgy Nut Coffee Pie, 52
Mint Chocolate Chip Pie, 49
Orange-Swirl Yogurt Pie, 55
Pumpkin Ice Cream Pie, 42
Soda Fountain Pie, 50
Strawberry Banana Pie, 103

Refrigerated
Banana Berry Tarts, 73
Blackberry Nectarine Pie, 57
Caramel-Pecan Cheese Pie, 59
Cherry Banana Cream Pie, 70
Chocolate-Caramel Supreme
    Pie, 98
Chocolate Cream Pie, 58
Coffee Mallow Pie, 62
Creamy Peanut Butter Pie, 60
Creamy Watermelon Pie, 63
Crown Jewel Gelatin Pie, 98
Fluffy Pineapple Pie, 62
Frosted Orange Pie, 58
Light Lemon Pie, 65
Red, White and Blueberry Pie, 102
Strawberry Chiffon Pie, 57
Summer Berry Cheese Pie, 71
Tin Roof Fudge Pie, 66
White Chocolate Pie, 73

PINEAPPLE
Fluffy Pineapple Pie, 62
Fruity Summer Cooler, 17
Lemon Pineapple Smoothies, 23
Orange Pineapple Smoothies, 29
Pineapple Ice Cream, 53
Pineapple Orange Sherbet, 42
Pineapple Smoothies, 22
Pineapple Sunrise Smoothies, 14
Sunny Slush, 26

Sweet Fruit Smoothies, 27
Three-Fruit Frozen Yogurt, 38
Tropical Milk Shakes, 6

PUDDING, MOUSSE & CREAM
Almond Creme, 78
Chilled Strawberry Cream, 77
Chocolate 'n' Toffee Rice
    Pudding, 88
Coffee Mousse, 91
Dark Chocolate Pudding, 78
Heavenly Chocolate Mousse, 85
Layered Banana Pudding, 83
Light Lemon Mousse, 80
Marshmallow Cream with Custard
    Sauce, 90
Melon Mousse, 82
Peach Mousse, 79
Peanut Butter Banana Pudding, 82
Pumpkin Mousse, 87
Raspberry Rice Pudding, 91
Raspberry White Chocolate
    Mousse, 97
Snowflake Pudding, 100
Walnut Pudding, 82

PUMPKIN
Frosty Ginger Pumpkin
    Squares, 102
Pumpkin Crunch Parfaits, 85
Pumpkin Ice Cream Pie, 42
Pumpkin Mousse, 87

RASPBERRIES
Angel Berry Trifle, 87
Banana Berry Tarts, 73
Berry Banana Smoothies, 30
Berry Smoothies, 21
Cherry Berry Smoothies, 29
Chocolate Raspberry Dessert, 38
Four-Berry Smoothies, 27
Four-Fruit Smoothies, 22
Frosty Freezer Pie, 33
Fruit Smoothies, 23
Fruity Red Smoothies, 7
Raspberry Chocolate Trifle, 85

Raspberry Cream Smoothies, 15
Raspberry Dessert with Vanilla
    Sauce, 61
Raspberry Ice Cream, 42
Raspberry Icebox Dessert, 66
Raspberry Lemon Smoothies, 25
Raspberry Rice Pudding, 91
Raspberry Smoothies, 7
Raspberry White Chocolate
    Mousse, 97
Snowflake Pudding, 100
Two-Tone Sherbet Torte, 95

REFRIGERATED DESSERTS
*(also see Cheesecakes; Parfaits;
Pies & Tarts; Pudding, Mousse &
Cream; Trifles)*

Apricot Delight, 75
Banana Cheesecake Dessert, 71
Black Forest Dessert, 60
Blueberry Angel Dessert, 60
Chocolate Cream Dessert, 74
Chocolate Mint Eclair Dessert, 75
Chocolate Mousse Loaf, 99
Coconut Angel Squares, 63
Cool Mandarin Dessert, 64
Cream Cheese Clouds, 105
Creamy Candy Bar Dessert, 72
Creamy Gelatin Dessert, 65
Creamy Strawberry Dessert, 63
Easy Tiramisu, 67
Lime Chiffon Dessert, 73
Make-Ahead Shortcake, 67
Peach Angel Dessert, 68
Peaches 'n' Cream Gelatin
    Dessert, 59
Raspberry Dessert with Vanilla
    Sauce, 61
Raspberry Icebox Dessert, 66
Strawberry Banana Dessert, 69

RHUBARB
Rhubarb Cheesecake Smoothies, 5
Rhubarb Gingersnap Parfaits, 86

RICE
Apricot Rice Custard, 84

ALPHABETICAL RECIPE INDEX

This handy index lists every recipe in alphabetical order, so you can quickly find your favorites.